D0875098

White on Black

Novel

RUBÉN DAVID GONSALES GALLEGO

Wild Leaf, Inc. Chicago, Illinois

ISBN: 978-965-92787-3-2
e-book ISBN: 978-965-92787-2-5

Published in the United States by
Wild Leaf, Inc.
www.wildleafgroup.com

Translated from Russian: Marian Schwartz
Edited by: Natalia Kucherova
Jacket design by: Natalia Kucherova
Jacket photographs: © Anne Yuyu

Manufactured in the United States of America

Books are available in quantity for promotional or premium use. For information on discounts and terms, please visit our website:
www.wildleafgroup.com

CONTENTS

Acknowledgments

Thanks to Eve, our Foremother, for eating the apple.
Thanks to Adam, for taking part.
Special thanks to Eve.

Thanks to my grandmother Esperanza for bearing my mama.
Thanks to Ignacio for taking part.
Special thanks to my grandmother.

Thanks to my mama for bearing me.
Thanks to David for taking part.
Special thanks to my mama.

Thanks to my mama for bearing my sister.
Thanks to Sergei for taking part.
Special thanks to my mama.

Thanks to my literature teacher. Once, when I was sick, she brought me chicken soup. She brought jam to class, and we ate the jam and were perfectly happy. When I wrote compositions, she gave me the highest mark, when she didn't give me the lowest.

Thanks to Sergei for editing and publishing my texts.
Special thanks to my literature teacher for the jam.

Thanks to my wives, for having been.
Thanks to my daughters, for have been and being.
Special thanks to my daughters for being.

Thanks to all the women, granddaughters and grandmothers, young and old, beautiful and less beautiful.

Thanks to all the men.

Special thanks to men for taking part.

Thanks again to my mama.

On Strength and Goodness

People sometimes ask me whether what I write actually happened. Are the characters of my stories real?

I answer: yes, it did, and yes, they are real—more than real. Naturally, my characters are collective images from the endless kaleidoscope of my endless orphanages. What I write, though, is the truth.

The sole characteristic of my work that departs from and sometimes even contradicts, the authenticity of real life is my authorial view, which may be rather sentimental, occasionally breaking into pathos. I purposely avoid writing about anything too terrible.

I am convinced that life and literature have more than enough of the dark side. It just so happened that I witnessed too much human cruelty and hate. To describe the vileness of man's downfall and bestiality is to multiply the already endless chain of interconnected blasts of evil. That's not what I want. I write about goodness, triumph, joy, and love.

I write about strength. Spiritual and physical strength. The strength that each one of us has inside. The strength that breaks through all barriers and leads to triumph. Every single one of my stories is a story of triumph. Even the boy from "The Cutlet," a rather sad story, is about triumphs. He has won twice. First, when out of the chaotic mess of his useless knowledge and lack of a knife, he finds the only three words that affect his adversary. And second, when he decides to eat the cutlets— that is, to live.

Those whose sole victory is their voluntary departure from life triumph as well. The officer who perishes in the face of a superior opponent, who dies according to the *Code of Conduct*[1], is victorious. I respect such people. All the same, what's most important about this man are the stuffed toys. I am convinced that sewing teddy bears and bunny rabbits all your life is much harder than slitting your throat once.

---

[1] Military Code of the Soviet Army. The law by which every soldier lives and dies

I am convinced that on humanity's scale a child's delight in a new toy vastly outweighs any military victory.

This is a book about my childhood. Cruel and terrible though it was, it was still my childhood. It doesn't take much for a child to retain his love for the world, grow up and mature: a bite of *lard*[1], a salami sandwich, a handful of figs, a blue sky, a couple of books and a kind word. That's enough—more than enough.

The characters of this book are strong, very strong people. All too often, a person has to be strong. And good. Not everyone can allow himself to be good, and not everyone can overcome universal misunderstandings. All too often, goodness is taken for weakness. That's sad. It's hard to be a human being, very hard, but altogether possible. And you don't have to stand on your hind legs to do it. Not at all. I believe that.

---

[1] Salted pork belly or "salo." Very popular in the Soviet Union, modern Russia, and Ukraine.

Hero

I am a hero. It's easy to be a hero. If you don't have arms or legs, you're either a hero or dead. If you don't have parents, rely on your arms and legs. And be a hero. If you don't have arms or legs and in addition, you have managed to enter this world an orphan—that's it. You are doomed to be a hero until the end of your days. Or you will kick the bucket. I am a hero. I have no other choice.

———— ◆ ————

I am a little boy. It's night. It is winter. I need to go to the toilet. Calling for an *attendant*[1] is pointless.

There is just one solution: I must crawl to the bathroom.

For starters, I have to get down from the bed. There is a way to do this; I came up with it myself. I just crawl to the edge of the bed, flip onto my back, and throw my body onto the floor. Wham! Pain.

I crawl to the door, push it open with my head and crawl out of the relatively warm room into the cold, dark hallway.

At night, all the windows in the hallway are left open. It's cold, very cold. I am naked.

It's a long way to crawl. When I pass the room where the attendants who look after us are sleeping, I call for help. I bang my head against the door. No response. I shout. No one. Maybe I am not crying loudly enough.

By the time I reach the bathroom, I am chilled to the bone.

The windows are open, and there's snow on the windowsill.

I reach the toilet. I rest. I absolutely must rest before crawling back. While I am resting, the pee in the toilet crusts over with ice.

I crawl back. I pull the blanket off the bed with my teeth, wrap myself up in it somehow, and try to fall asleep.

---

[1] Soviet orphanage attendant, low-payed nanny, and warden. Most of them do not have a proper education

———— ◆ ————

In the morning, they dress me and take me to school. In history class, I confidently recount the horrors of Nazi concentration camps. I get the top mark. I always get the top marks in history. I have top marks in all my subjects. I am a hero.

The Bayonet

The bayonet is an excellent thing. Reliable. One blow and your opponent falls. A bayonet pierces straight through your enemy's body. A bayonet never lets you down; a bayonet kills for sure. A bullet kills at random; a bullet is a fool. A bullet might pass through on a tangent. A bullet can get stuck in the body and meanly, from the inside, eat human life. A bayonet is not a bullet. A bayonet is cold steel, the last relic of the nineteenth century.

There is a bayonet embossed on the cover of Nikolai Ostrovsky's[1] first book. The blind, paralyzed writer could not read his own book. All he had left was running his fingers over and over the bayonet's contours. The most durable bayonet in the world is a bayonet made of paper.

The ancient Vikings were the best fighters in the world. Fearless warriors, real men, strong of spirit. It is too early to discard a Viking who fell in battle. In the last impulse of his passing life, a Viking who fell in battle would sink his teeth into his enemy's leg. Dying slowly, cursing your good-for-nothing life, and exasperating yourself and the people close to you with endless complaints about your luckless fate is the lot of the weak. A soldier in battle doesn't care about Hamlet's timeless question. Living in combat and dying in combat are the same thing. To live half-heartedly and die half-heartedly or pretentiously is repugnant and vile. The greatest thing a mortal can hope for is to go down fighting. If he is lucky, if he is fortunate, he can die fighting. Die clutching a horse's bridle or the controls of a fighter plane, a saber or a machine gun, a blacksmith's hammer, or a chess king. If they chop your hand off in battle, it's not a calamity. You can pick up the blade with your other hand. If it falls, all is not yet lost. There is still a chance, a small chance of dying like a Viking, of clenching your enemy's heel with your teeth. Not everyone is that lucky; not everyone gets to do this. Homer and Beethoven are the rare exceptions that only confirm the remoteness of

---

[1] Soviet writer. His novel, "The Making of a Hero," is a fictionalized autobiography

the odds. But you have to fight. There is no other choice; any other way is dishonest and stupid.

I cried over a book. Books, like people, can be different. If you think hard about it, comic books are books too—beautiful books with beautiful pictures. Entertaining toys—paper butterflies that live for one day—comic books have an enormous advantage over all other books in that they don't make children cry. Books shouldn't make happy little children cry. "To be or not to be" has no meaning for them. They are children, just little kids. It's too early for them to be thinking. I read the book. I read it, and I cried. I cried out of impotence and envy. I wanted to be there. I wanted to fight, but I couldn't. I couldn't do anything. I was used to that, but even so, I cried. Some books change the way you look at the world, books that make you want to live, or die differently.

If you want to understand something, you have to ask either people or books. Books are people, too. Like people, books can help. Like people, books lie.

I wasn't simply reading books. I was trying to understand how the world works. I wanted to find out how I was supposed to live in this world. I asked people, but they wouldn't tell me. I searched for the answer in books, and the books ducked the question. The books told in detail, in great detail, how to live if you have everything. Book heroes suffered, which amazed me. I, a real living person, did not understand them, these fictional people. I didn't accept their paper sufferings. They were pretending, like the teachers at school. The teachers advised me to read books, and I did. I read one book after another. I read endless tedious descriptions of the pointless lives of weak and lazy people. The teachers called these people heroes, but I couldn't understand what their heroism consisted of.

Is d'Artagnan a hero? What kind of hero could he be if he had arms and legs? He had everything—youth, health, beauty, a saber, and an ability to fence. Where is the heroism in that? A coward and a traitor who is repeatedly committing foolish acts just for glory and riches–is that a hero? I read the book without understanding even half. Everyone—adults and children alike—considered the musketeers as heroes. I didn't argue. Arguing was pointless. In any case, I couldn't use these heroes as my role models.

I read this thick book end-to-end several times. I also read the continuation of the famous tale of the brave musketeers. The continuation did not disappoint me. The unlucky freak, Monsieur Coquenard did what a real hero was supposed to do: he died. He died, leaving his wife and his money to Porthos. Monsieur Coquenard did not arouse my sympathy, though. If that pathetic old man had the strength and the smarts to sprinkle poison into Porthos' wine, I would have been on his side. But there are no miracles. The unfortunate cripple dragged out his miserable existence, proving a background with his invalid's chair on which the true heroes' deeds could shine brighter. Poor fellow.

The others were no better. Pathetic little people worthy of contempt. Insects who resembled people only in part. Shitbags not good enough for heaven or hell. Warriors who didn't know how to live or die. Only a few of them earned my respect to any extent. Porthos, for instance. I liked Porthos much better than Coquenard. Porthos at least managed to die like a man.

Gwynplaine was a fool who suffered over nothing. Imagine a disfigured face. Cyrano behaved a little more intelligently. If you have two strong hands and a sharp sword, beauty can be debated. And a sword is not a bad argument. Actually, Cyrano disappointed me too. Strong in his dealings with men, he turned out to be a sniveler and a whiner in the face of love.

I envied Quasimodo. People looked at him with disgust and pity, the same way they looked at me. But he had arms and legs. He had all of the Notre Dame de Paris. Book heroes weren't heroes, or they were heroes only in part. The very best of them behaved like men from time to time, but reluctantly, I thought. They allowed themselves to live only a few minutes before they died. Only just before they died did I like them. Only a worthy death reconciled them to their pointless life.

Rarely did I cry over books. I had plenty of reasons to cry without some invented book grief. But one book was the real thing. One book didn't lie.

Pavka Korchagin[1] galloped on horseback and wielded a blade just as well as the musketeers. Pavka Korchagin was a strong, brave fellow. He fought for an idea; he did not care for money or promotions. His Red Army helmet—bearing a pitiful resemblance to a knight's—couldn't protect him from a crude bullet. His sharp blade was powerless against a Mauser pistol. He knew this, but he went into combat. He went into the fray over and over again. Over and over again, he rushed into the very thick of battle. He fought and won, always won. He triumphed with a weapon and a word. When his body gave out when his hand could no longer hold a blade, he changed weapons, and his pen became his

---

[1] A fictional character of Nikolai Ostrovsky's novel "The Making of a Hero," based on the author's own experience

bayonet. He managed to do that. The last knight of cold steel. The last Viking of the twentieth century.

What does a man have left when he has almost nothing? How can he justify the pathetic quasi existence of his quasi corpse? Why should he live? I didn't know then, and I don't know now. Like Pavel Korchagin, though, I do not want to die before my death. I want to live to the very end. I am going to put up a fight. Slowly pressing the computer keys, I type letter by letter. I am painstakingly forging my own bayonet—my book. I know I have the right to just one strike; there will not be any second chance for me. I am trying, trying hard. I know that bayonet kills for sure. A bayonet is an excellent thing. Reliable.

Dreams

When I was little, I dreamed of my mama. I dreamed of her until I was six. Then I realized—or more likely, it was explained to me—that my mommy was a black-assed bitch who has abandoned me. I don't enjoy writing this, but they explained the situation to me in precisely those terms.

The people who did the explaining were big and strong, and they were right about everything. Therefore, they were also right about such a trifle. Of course, there were other grownups as well.

There were the teachers. The teachers told me stories about faraway lands and great writers, about how life was wonderful, and every person would find himself a place in the world if only he studied well and obeyed his elders. Of course, they were always lying, and they lied about everything. They told stories about stars and continents, but they wouldn't let me out of the *children's home*[1] gates. They talked about all people's equality, but only the "walking[2]" kids were allowed to go to the circus and the movies.

The attendants were the only ones who didn't lie. In Russian orphanages, the attendants were called by a wonderful word: "Nyanya[3]." A sweet word that immediately calls to mind Pushkin's famous line, "Let's drink, Nyanya..." Down-to-earth, hardworking women. They never lied. Once in a while, they even treated us to candy. Some were mean, and some had good hearts, but they were all direct and sincere. Often you could extract the essence of something from what they said when it was impossible to get an intelligible answer from the teachers. When they gave you a piece of candy, they would say: "Poor child, better you'd died. You would have spared the suffering both yourself and us as well". Or, when they were carrying out someone who

---

[1] In this book, children's home is housing for kids with disabilities, even ones who have parents, an isolated state institution.

[2] Ambulant or "walking" ones are ambulatory patients: the kids or elderly who can walk on their own

[3] A nanny. Low paid service staff member, a babysitter, and a cleaning person. Usually, old low-educated women took this job.

died: "Thank God, his suffering is over, poor thing." Whenever I caught a cold and didn't have to go to school, I was left in the sleeping wing with one of these attendants. The good-hearted woman would bring me something sweet or some of her stewed fruit and tell about her children killed in the war, her drunk of a husband, and other interesting things. I listened and believed everything, the way children—and only children, perhaps—can accept the truth. Grownups cannot believe in anything anymore. So, you see, the attendants told me about the black-assed bitch so casually and naturally, as if they were talking about rain or snow.

At the age of six, I stopped dreaming of my mama. I dreamed of becoming a walking one. Almost everyone could walk, even those who could barely get around on crutches. The walkers were treated much better than we were. They were human beings. After they graduated from the children's home, they could become useful for society— bookkeepers, shoemakers, weavers. Many graduates received a good education and "become somebody." They would come to visit us driving expensive cars. Then we would assemble in the auditorium, and they told us about their career: where they are working and in what position. These stories implied that these fat, middle-aged men and women had always obeyed the elders, studied well, and earned everything by their wits and persistence. But they could walk! What kind of moron did I have to be to listen to their boastful talk if I knew very well what you were supposed to do after you became a walking-able? But no one ever explained to me how to become one.

When I was eight, I understood the very simple idea: I am alone, and nobody needs me. Grownups and children alike think only of themselves. Naturally, I knew that somewhere on another planet, there were mammas, daddies, and grandmas and grandpas. But that was so far away and unconvincing that I relegated these fantasies to the sphere of stars and continents.

At the age of nine, I understood that I was never going to walk. That was very sad. Distant lands, stars, and other joys were cut off to me. The only thing left was death-a long and useless death.

When I was ten, I read about the kamikazes. These bold fellows inflicted death on the enemy. By a single one-way flight, they repaid all the debts to their homeland: for all the rice they had eaten, for the diapers they'd soiled, for school notebooks, for the girls' smiles, for the sun and stars, for the right to see their mama every day. That suited me. I realized no one was ever going to let me on an airplane. I dreamed of a torpedo—a guided torpedo filled with explosives. I dreamed of sneaking up to an enemy aircraft carrier very quietly and pressing the red button.

Many years have passed since then. I am a grown man now, and I understand everything. Maybe that's good, but perhaps that's not so good. Most of the people who understand everything are boring and primitive. I have no right to wish for death because my family's destiny largely depends on me. My wife and children love me, and I love them very, very much. Sometimes, though, when I lie in bed, unable to fall asleep, I still dream of the torpedo and the red button. This naïve, childish dream has never left me, and probably never will.

Food

I didn't like to eat. If I could have, I would have preferred pills like the ones in science fiction stories. I would have swallowed a pill like that and been full all day. I ate poorly, and they were always coaxing me, spoon-feeding me. It was all useless. I was lucky when I was very little. I lived in a small children's home out in the countryside. They fed me well, and the food was delicious. The attendants were kind. They always made sure all the children ate well and cared about us.

Later there were other children's homes, other attendants, and other food. We have seen pearl barley, wormy biscuits, rotten eggs. We had it all. But I am going to write about something else.

I catch myself thinking that my best memories are connected with food. All the best moments of my childhood are associated with food, or rather, with the people who shared food with me, who gave me food, as a token of goodwill. It's odd.

———— ◆ ————

I don't remember where this was. I do remember people in white lab coats. There were lots of us children, and we all were very small.

They brought a pineapple into the room. I thought it was very big and beautiful. They didn't cut it up right away, but let us admire it. The grownups apparently couldn't bring themselves to destroy this beauty. Pineapples are rare in Russia.

The pineapple disappointed everyone. Or rather, nearly everyone. The children all tried its sharp, peculiar taste and refused to eat these stinging slices. Only I ate them. I remember the grownups' conversation:

"Let's give him more."

"What's the matter with you? What if it makes him sick?"

"Have you seen his chart? I'll bet his father grew up on these pineapples. Maybe they have pineapples there the way we have potatoes."

They gave me more and more. The grownups must have found it amusing the way this odd child could eat this exotic fruit. And they couldn't bring themselves to throw out so much of value. I ate many slices of pineapple. And I didn't get sick.

———— ◆ ————

They brought me to my first children's home. There were no people in white lab coats or rows of beds. On the other hand, there were lots of children and a TV set.

"What, you mean he can't sit at all? Let's put him up on the couch and prop him up with pillows."

They put me on the couch, propped me up with pillows, and fed me cream of wheat by a spoon. I was so surprised that I ate a whole plate and fell asleep. The cream of wheat was delicious. I liked this children's home."

———— ◆ ————

The hospital. Night-time. Everyone's asleep. A nurse runs into the ward and turns on the night-light over my bed. She is wearing a fancy dress and high heels, and her hair is lying loose on her shoulders. She bends low over me. Her eyes are very big and happy. She smells of perfume and something else, from home, not the hospital.

"Open your mouth and close your eyes."

I comply. She puts a big piece of chocolate in my mouth. I know how you are supposed to eat chocolates. You are supposed to hold the chocolate and take little bites. Not only that, but I wanted to get a better look at this candy.

"Chew it up and swallow. Okay?"

I nod.

She turns off the night-light and runs out. I chew up the candy. My mouth fills with something sweet and stinging. I am chewing the chocolate, and for some reason, my head is spinning. I feel good. Happy.

———— ◆ ————

They've moved me to another children's home. I am crawling down the hallway, and an attendant is walking towards me. It's dark in the hall, and she doesn't notice me right away. When she gets very close, she suddenly shrieks and jumps back. Then she comes closer and bends down to get a better look at me. I have swarthy skin, and my head is shaved. At first glance, in the dim light of the hallway, all you can see are my eyes, my big eyes, suspended in the air six inches off the floor.

"You are really thin. Nothing but skin and bones. Like he just got out of Buchenwald."

It's true, I am not very fat. They didn't feed me very well at the place they brought me from, and I ate poorly anyway.

She walks away. She comes back a couple of minutes later and puts a piece of bread and lard on the floor in front of me. That is the first lard I've seen in my life, which is why I eat the salo first and then the bread. Suddenly I feel all warm and cozy, and I drift off to sleep.

———— ◆ ————

It's Easter. All the attendants are dressed up festively. There is a feeling of holiday in everything: in the fact that the attendants are especially kind to us, and the teacher aides are extra watchful. I don't understand anything. You see, during holidays, they show parades and marches on television. Only on New Year's there is no parade. But when it is a New Year, there is a Christmas tree and presents.

After breakfast, an attendant gives each of us a dyed egg. Inside, the egg is white, like a regular egg. I eat the whole Easter egg. It's delicious, much tastier than the eggs they give to us at the children's home. Those eggs were overcooked and hard, but this one is soft and very, very tasty.

Oddly enough, no matter where I was, whether in a children's home, a hospital, or an old folks' home, some good souls always gave me a dyed egg at Easter. And that is just great.

———— ◆ ————

In Russia, there's a custom of honoring the dead by sharing food. On the fortieth day after someone dies, his relatives are supposed to share food, but not just with anyone. They have to bring it to those who are most miserable. The more unfortunate the person is fed, the more you've pleased the deceased, and the greater is your merit before God. But where was one to find them, the unfortunates, in the most fortunate country in the world? And so they came to the gate of our children's home, poor devils, with their bags, baskets, and packages. They brought candies, cookies, and buns. They brought pirozhki and blini—whatever they could. All the attempts of our indefatigable teacher aides to keep them away were mostly unsuccessful.

Taking advantage of their official position, our attendants would bring the "funeral food" through the children's home gate, despite a strict official ban. Most of the luck had the attendants who worked with us, the non-walkers. We were fed separately, and the teacher aides were far away. One attendant cleverly slipped a pot of fruit jelly through the front door. Not only that, but since we were the most miserable of all, the candies fed to us had much bigger spiritual value.

For our part, we knew that we were not supposed to say thank you for the funeral food and that when they gave you these treats, you weren't supposed to smile.

I was lying in the garden. "The garden" was what we called the few apple trees that grew next to the home. It took me a long time to crawl to the garden, so I was tired and lying on my back, resting. All the "walking ones" were far away, watching a movie at the club, maybe. They'd been taken somewhere—I don't remember where. I was lying there waiting for an apple to fall, not too far away. But I had much better luck than that.

A withered old woman was clambering over the fence. The fence was two meters high, but that didn't stop the granny. She hopped down, looked both ways, and walked towards me. After soberly examining my arms and legs, she asked tentatively, "An orphan, surely?". I nodded. Such luck she had never anticipated: crooked arms and legs and also an orphan. She put her basket on the ground, threw back the towel covering the contents, took out a blin, gave it to me, and commanded, "Eat." I quickly began eating blini while she hurried me along, repeating: "Auntie Varvara, pray for Auntie Varvara". But all good things end quickly. A teacher aide was walking toward us.

"Why are there outsiders on the grounds? Who let her in? What are you doing here?"

And then to me:

"What are you doing?"

What was I doing? I was chewing on my third blin. I was chewing fast because I still had half a blin in my hand, and I wanted to finish all of it.

The nimble granny already snatched her basked and hurdled over the fence. I quickly finished the blin. The teacher aide stood there for a while, then smiled at something and walked away.

These were the first blini I'd eaten in my life.

———— ◆ ————

They are moving me again from one children's home to another. The fun begins at the train station, where they give me ice cream and lemon soda. The ice-cream bar is big and coated with chocolate. As soon as the train starts moving, the attendant and the nurse go off "for a stroll", as they put it. "Hey, go for a stroll?" They come back with two Georgians. One Georgian is old and grey. The other is a little younger. They are all drinking vodka and having a good time. They cut me a big hunk of sausage; they give me hard-boiled eggs and lemon soda. The grey-haired Georgian keeps cutting sausage, making sandwiches, and telling me: "Go ahead, eat! Children should eat well". There is an awful lot of food, and no one is keeping track of it. It's getting dark, and I can look out the window all I want and eat sausage. I feel like riding and riding and looking out the window. I think about how if all the grownups on earth were given a lot of vodka and sausage, they would be kind, and all the children would be happy.

———— ◆ ————

I am in my last children's home, the best children's home in the world. In front of me is my breakfast: a little mashed potato, a lovely tomato half, a buttered roll, and tea. I know for sure that today isn't a holiday, so why did they give me potatoes then? I try the tea: it's sweet. A fresh tomato is a delicacy in itself. I eat it all and realize that I have had fantastic luck. I've landed in paradise.

———— ◆ ————

Katya and I are living in a half-basement because her parents won't recognize our marriage. The apartment belongs to my teacher, one of the finest women on earth. She let us live in her apartment while she has moved to live at her dacha.

On her way home from the university, Katya buys pelmeni. She cooks the whole package at once. I know what pelmeni are—little dough balls filled with meat. They used to give them to us at the children's home, four per kid.

"How many are we each going to eat?"—I ask Katya.

She gives me a strange look.

"What, you mean? Have you counted them?"

Katya serves us pelmeni. She eats a plate of them, but I can't get down more than six. I realize that in this strange, unregimented world, people don't count pelmeni.

"Don't throw out the pelmeni water," I advise Katya practically. "You can use it to make soup."

A few days later, we are visiting her parents, and Katya is eating pelmeni again. Her mama takes a pot off the table and is about to go to the kitchen.

"Mama, don't pour out the water, you can use it to make soup," Katya says automatically.

The next day, when Katya leaves for classes at the university, her mom tiptoes up to our building and leaves a fresh chicken by the door. The ice has been broken.

———— ◆ ————

When Katya leaves for work, I am left one on one with the most enchanting of women. We are living in an apartment with her grandmother.

She stops by the room and sits down, facing me.

"Well, so when are you going to croak?"

"Hold your horses," I reply. "I will croak when it is my time. You are no spring chicken yourself. Or are you planning on living forever?"

"Who needs you when you are so useless, no arms, no legs? You can't even hammer a nail."

"Do you have a marking pen?"

"Yes."

"You go all through the apartment, and everywhere you need a nail, put a mark. Believe me, the nails will get hammered in."

And so we pass the time in a heart-to-heart conversation. Grandma tells me about her youth and her relatives. Her stories lead me to believe that her entire clan is nothing but a bunch of rogues and scoundrels.

After a while, she goes into the kitchen and rattles the pots. She comes in.

"Ruben, I made borscht. Are you going to eat it, or are you afraid I'll poison you?"

"Let's have the borscht. I am not afraid of being poisoned. I have eaten worse."

She brings me the borscht. The borscht is delicious. At the bottom of the plate is a big piece of duck meat.

———— ◆ ————

When Alla was pregnant, we were living hand to mouth. Alla ate bread with cooking lard. I couldn't eat lard; I ate bread and sunflower oil. (In children's homes, bread drizzled with sunflower oil and sprinkled with salt was considered a treat.) That year, for the first time, I had trouble with my digestion. We were also making pea soup. Alla didn't eat soup, and I ate nothing else. It was a hundred times easier for me than for her; I could eat soup, and I wasn't pregnant. When Maya was born, Alla decided to breastfeed her. Natural nourishment is very healthy. But Maya wasn't eating well, and Alla's milk was greenish. And so was Maya's poop. All this time, Alla was eating nothing but potatoes. Alla is a healthy person, and she needs a lot more food than I do. What she consumes in one meal I eat in a day. We decided that switching Maya to the formula would be cheaper than providing Alla with proper nourishment.

———— ◆ ————

A friend came over.

"How are you doing?"

"Fine."

"What are you eating?"

"A pea soup."

"With potatoes?"

"Naturally."

"We've been eating pea soup without potatoes for more than a week."

I have been eating pea soup for just three days. I have a sack of potatoes.

———— ◆ ————

Maya is one and a half. She refused to eat her hot cereal. I take it and calmly finish it. Maya asked for some sausage first, then gingerbread. We don't have either one, but that's not the point. If you are hungry, you will eat what's available; if not, then run along (a children's home rule). Maya walks around the apartment and thinks. Then she calmly goes over to Alla and says: "Mama, cook potatoes." We eat potatoes with salt and sunflower oil, and I remember how in the children's home, we cooked potatoes after lights out with the help of a jerry-rigged immersion heater. The things I didn't get until I was fifteen (only high-school students could cook potatoes), Maya already had from birth.

———— ◆ ————

Alla brings Maya home from nursery school. Alla is laughing. She ran into the cook, who proudly told her that there was a chicken for lunch today at kindergarten. "It was so big and fat that everyone got a piece." There more than a hundred children at the nursery school. And there was one chicken, or rather one and a half. I laugh too.

I am glad that Maya is attending nursery school. She has lots of friends there, and they sculpt with playdough and paint pictures. Not only that but when she comes home from nursery school, Maya eats what she is given and doesn't fuss.

———— ◆ ————

On the way home from nursery school, Maya asks Alla to buy her some rusks.

"What's the matter with you? We have money now. If you want, I will buy you a pastry or anything else."

"No, I want rusks."

Alla buys the rusks. Maya sits down at the table and gnaws away at her rusks all evening. It turns out, at snack time, the teachers had given the children a rusk apiece, and Maya wanted more. At the children's home, they gave us two rusks apiece.

———— ◆ ————

When I was living at the old folks' home, one thing amazed me. In the dining room after the midday meal, they would pass out the bones. These were ordinary beef bones from the soup. Only war veterans were supposed to get bones. The meat had been carefully cut off the bones, but you could still get more if you are deft enough. The veterans crowded in front of the wicket, cursed, and shouted out their merits and service records. Recently I asked my friend from the school whether they still gave out bones there.

"What's the matter with you? They haven't cooked anything with bones for a long time. There are no bones."

The Nannies

There were very few of them. Genuine "nyanyas"—caring attendants, full of kindness and concern. I don't remember their names, or rather, I don't remember all the names of all the good-hearted ones. Among ourselves, we divided them up into "evil" and "good". In that children's world, the line between good and evil seemed obvious. For a long time, I've tried—unsuccessfully—to shake the bad habit acquired in children's home of dividing people into us and them, smart and stupid, good and evil. What can I do? I grew up where there was a fine line between life and death, and where meanness and nastiness were standard. So were sincerity and goodness. It was all a jumble. The constant need to choose bad and good must have fostered this categorical streak in me.

The good attendants believed in God. All of them. There, I have gone and divided up people into categories again. I can't seem to get away from it.

Believing in God was forbidden. They told us that there was no God. Atheism was the norm. Nowadays, hardly anyone would believe this, but that's how it was. I don't know whether any of the teachers believed in God. There probably were some. The teachers were forbidden to talk to us about that. Making the sign of a cross or dying an Easter egg could get the teacher fired—but not an attendant. An attendant's wages were low, and there was a lot of work. There weren't many people eager to wash floors and change children's pants. The management simply turned a blind eye to believing attendants. So attendants stick to their faith. They believed in God no matter what. They prayed for a long time when they were on night duty, lighting a candle they'd brought along. They made the sign of the cross over us at night. At Easter, they brought us dyed eggs and blini. It was forbidden to bring food into the children's home, but what could the strict administrators do to those illiterate women?

There were just a few good attendants. I remember them all. Right now, I will try to tell a story about one of them. This is a real story, one

of the attendants told me. I will try to retell what my childish memory
retained, as accurately as I can.

———— ◆ ————

"I've been working here for a long time. When I arrived, I looked, and
there were little children, some without legs, some without arms. And
everyone was dirty. You wash one, then he crawls across the floor—and
he's dirty again. Some you have to spoon-feed, some you have to wash
every hour. I was so tired. On the first night shift, I did not lie down for
a minute. They'd brought in a new one, and he kept calling his mama all
night long. I sat by his bed, took his hand, and stayed like that with him
until morning. I cried and cried. In the morning, I went to the priest and
asked for his blessing to quit. "I can't do it"—I said—"I can't watch this.
I feel so sorry for everyone. It breaks my heart." But the priest wouldn't
give his blessing. He said, "This is your cross to the end of your days." I
begged and pleaded with him. But then I worked for a while and learned
to live with it. It is still hard. I write down the names of the children I
take care of on a piece of paper. I have a notebook at home, and that's
where I write all of you down. And at Easter, I light a candle for each one
of you. It's getting to be a lot of candles. It's expensive. But still, I light
one, and I say an Our Father for each one of you. Because the Lord told
us to pray for all the innocent children. But you have such a strange
name, Ruben. Must be Armenian. The Armenians are Christians—I
know that. Not Armenian, you say? Then I thought, since his parents
don't come to visit, his parents must be Basurmans or something. A
christened soul wouldn't abandon her child. They are bitches. God
forgive me, old fool that I am. No matter how hard I try not to sin, but I
cannot help it. But you are going to be in my notebook without the last
name recorded. Your last name is so queer, and I wouldn't be able to
write it. Everyone is written down with a last name except you. In
prayer, you are only supposed to say the first name, but it's still not right
that there is no last name.

———— ◆ ————

What can I add to this story? I grew up, read tons of different books, and
now I think I am very smart. Thank you to my teachers, who taught me
how to read. Thank you to the Soviet state that raised me. Thank you to

the smart Americans who created the computer and gave me the chance to type this text with my left index finger.

Thank you to all the good-hearted attendants for teaching me about kindness and the warmth in my heart that I carried through all my trials. Thank you for what can't be expressed in words, or entered on a computer, or measured. Thank you for your love and Christian mercy, for the fact that I am a Catholic, and for my little children. For everything.

The Lads

There were ten of us in the ward. Or rather, nine. We didn't count Vovochka. Vovochka couldn't talk. He couldn't do anything, only eat and shit. Often, he woke us up with his yelling. As always, he was hungry. He could eat a lot, however much they gave him. They gave him the same as everyone else, but that wasn't enough for him, and he would yell. That was a twelve-year-old baby.

There was also me and Vasilek. Vasilek looked twenty. He had paralyzed legs. He was as strong as an ox. Or rather, he was as fit as most of the mentally disabled people. Once, he grabbed the attendant who was teasing him by the leg, and she couldn't escape. The bruise on her leg took a very long time to heal. The attendants tease him, the harmless bull, and gave him a smack on the back as they walked by or said something dirty, and then he would jack off noisily all night long, providing grounds for new jokes. However, they treated him well and always served him a double portion.

I am a nine-year-old boy. Imagine a paralyzed little person lying on the floor, his upper body propped up on his elbows and rocking from side to side. He is doing something, but you can't quite tell what. He is crawling. I crawled fast. In half an hour, I could crawl three hundred meters if I wasn't tired. Though every ten or fifteen meters, I had to rest. But I could crawl! Vasilek and I were the only ones in the ward who could crawl. That's what distinguished us from the rest.

There were seven of them. I don't remember all the names. Not that I was supposed to know their names. Only Sashka Poddubny could sit up. Every morning the attendants would seat him on the floor in front of the low table. The rest lay in their beds around the clock. We called them "the lads." The respect for them in the children's home was absolute; even the head honcho would come to consult with them. We were the only ones with the television in our room, and we could watch it whenever we wanted.

I ended up in that ward by chance. When they brought me, one of the lads had just died. Thus was unlucky bunk number three. Three boys occupied it before me. They are all dead now. No one wanted to take this bunk, but I was a new kid. Then they tried to move me to another ward, but Sashka Poddubny asked them to keep me there. That's another story.

———— ◆ ————

One day Sashka needed to go to the toilet, but Vasilek wasn't in the room.

I had a choice: crawl after an attendant or try to help him myself. I grabbed the elastic of his pants with my teeth, pulled back, pushed the pot, and he peed. Now, according to the unspoken rule of the children's home, I could ask him a favor, too. I summoned all my nerve and asked him to let me read one of his books. He had a lot of books. He was constantly reading something or translating from German.

"Take The Three Musketeers." He said.

"I've already read it, and it is for children, give me Solaris[1]."

"You won't understand anything in it."

"Yes, I will."

"You're stubborn, that's good. Take Solaris and then tell me what you understood."

I read Solaris in one Sunday. When Sashka asked me what I'd understood from the book, I replied, "It was stupid for the main character to fly off, because he should have cleared things up with the woman, on Earth, first." Sashka said that I was still little and didn't understand anything. But after that, he started lending me books. All in all, I was lucky. The lads treated me well.

———— ◆ ————

The volunteers came to see us. Our volunteers were students from the teacher's college.

They assembled us in the auditorium, and our volunteers sang little songs for us and left. Or rather, not everyone left. According to the volunteer schedule, students had to do certain activities with us, help us with our lessons, etc. But most of them looked at us as if we were lepers. This expression "as if they were lepers" I read later, and I liked it a lot.

---

[1] Solaris is the philosophical sci-fi novel by Polish writer Stanislaw Lem.

How else can I convey their bugged-out eyes and poorly concealed disgust?

Some did come, though. Strangely, it was the female students who weren't exactly setting the world on fire. Innate goodness and compassion, maybe curiosity, too, brought them to see us over and over again.

One of the girls stopped in to visit.

"Boys, can I help you with anything?"

"Want some chifir[1]?" He asked casually.

"What?"

"A strong tea."

"Sure."

"Then get me the kettle from under our mattress and the can from the night table, go get some water and set it all up under the bed." That was Vovka-Moscow talking. That was his nickname: "Moscow." Why? I don't know.

The student visited us several times, and the lads treated her with chocolates and badgered her with jokes. It was nice and fun to be around her.

One day she stayed longer than usual, and it was time for her to get home. Naturally, no one wanted to let her go.

"Boys, I have to do my physics and math, and it's not something I can just dash off."

"What grade are you in?"

"Sophomore."

"Do you have your textbooks with you?"

"Yes, in my bag."

"Get it out and read a problem." That was Genka, talking from the corner bed.

She did and sat down to read.

"But I don't understand any of it."

"Me neither. I've only been studying that stuff for a year. Read it out loud."

"The formulas too?" She asked.

"Yes, the formulas too."

---

[1] An extremely strong tea. It is popular in Soviet and Russian prisons as one of the affordable ways to get high.

She read her textbooks, and we rejoiced that she still hadn't left. We were confident that Genka would solve all her problems.

She read for a long time, and then Genka told her to sit down at the table and write.

"But you can't see what I am writing."

"But you can, can't you?" Genka asked.

"Yes."

"Well then, write."

He dictated the solutions to all her problems, then fell silent.

"Can I check the answers? I have the answers written out here."

"Go ahead."

"It all matches! How did you do that? Without looking at my notebook. You are so little!"

Genka weighed ten kilos. Not only could he not walk, but there was also something wrong with his thyroid, and he didn't grow. Usually, they pulled a blanket up to his chin, and the face of an eight-year-old boy looked out. However, that was for the best. Occasionally they carried him outside. Vasilek and I could crawl onto the pavement by ourselves while others have never been outside.

"I am eighteen. I am as 'little' as you."

"Oh, boys" (she called them boys, which no one else did). "And I thought you were still in elementary school."

"Officially, we are in second grade. But some of us have stayed in the same class for two years. That's just because we have a children's home director with a good heart. He doesn't want to cart us off to the old folks' home. There'd be no one to take care of us there, and we'd die."

"But why don't you go to college? You would be top students."

"They only accept walking ones into college."

She gathered her things very quickly and left. I crawled out into the hallway. It was raining, and I wanted to crawl to the main door.

It was chilly—late autumn or early spring. They never shut the main door, and I liked to crawl right up to the entrance and watch the rain. Occasional drops of rain would fall inside, fall on me. It felt good and sad.

That time, though, my place by the door was taken.

Leaning heavily against the door frame stood that same student, smoking greedily, taking deep drags. And she was crying. I don't remember what she was wearing. All I remember is her high-heeled shoes. She was beautiful. I thought I would never see such a pretty girl again. She was smoking and crying. Then she finished her cigarette and went out into the rain, without a raincoat or umbrella.

She stopped coming to see us.

———— ◆ ————

A commission arrived from Moscow. The director was reprimanded. All the boys were taken away to a nursing home. The lads' teacher aide came to see us in our classroom. "From now on, I am going to work with you until you graduate." I started fifth grade that year, elementary school was over, and now we were supposed to have "our" classroom teacher and "our" teacher aide.

A month after the lads were taken to the old folks' home, she visited her former students. She came back and told us everything.

Out of eight of them, only Genka survived. The old folks' home consisted of separate barrack-type buildings. The elderly and the handicapped were distributed according to their degree of disability. Our lads were placed to separate barracks with the "goners." Urine dripped from their beds, which were stretched out in rows along the walls. No one came near them. The teacher aide had brought them big cans of compote. Here is what she said about Genka: "He is some angry." "Take the compote back," he says. "The walking ones are going to take it anyway."

I asked her what would happen to me when I grow up. Will they take me to an old folks' home, too, and will I die?

"Yes, of course." She replied.

"But I'll be fifteen; I don't want to die so soon. Does that mean it's all for nothing? Why should I study, then?"

"Nothing is for nothing. You have to study because they feed you for free. And anyway, have you done your homework?"

Since then, I have changed dramatically. Any small thing could make me cry. They tried to console me or even making threats of punishments. Nothing worded. I screamed at the top of my lungs.

They called in the doctor. A young fellow arrived, sat down in front of me on the floor, smiled, and asked me something. I smiled back. I didn't want to talk to him, but finally, I had to.

"Why do you cry so often?" Doctor asked.

"I don't cry often."

"Why did you cry yesterday?"

"I was crawling around, I hit my head, and I started crying."

"I don't believe you. Your teacher aide told me everything. You cry all the time. That's not normal. Why don't you want to talk to me?"

"Because you are a psychiatrist. They are all so nice in the beginning, but then they take you away to the hospital. And in the hospital, they give you shots, and they give you pills to make you like Vasilek."

"Who told you that nonsense? No one is going to take you away. And who's this Vasilek?"

"Vovka-Moscow told me about the hospital."

"And where is your Vovka now?"

"He is dead. They are all dead. They were good and smart. And Sashka Poddubny lent me nice books to read. Now they are gone, but Vasilek is alive. They took him to a different children's home, a good one. Because he can crawl and go to the toilet by himself."

"Who told you they all died?"

"The teacher aide. She also told me they're going to take me away too. It will happen when I am fifteen. I am ten now."

The smiling teacher aide looked at the doctor perplexedly and said: "Well, so what? What is the problem? I told this to the whole." The doctor lit a cigarette. That was the first time I'd ever seen an adult smoke right in the ward. For some reason, I liked him.

"Are you afraid of me?" He asked.

"Yes."

He wasn't scary at all. He finished his cigarette, looked at me, and left.

Genka died very soon after.

America

We were supposed to hate that country. That was the custom. We were supposed to hate all capitalist countries, especially America. Our enemies—the bourgeoisie, who drank the blood of the working class—lived in America. American imperialism was making the atomic bomb with our name on it. The workers in America were always starving and dying. And an endless stream of people hoping to change their citizenship kept pouring into the Soviet embassy in the United States. That's what they taught us, and we believed it.

I loved America. I'd loved it since I was nine. I was nine when they told me there are no disabled people in America. Because they are killed. All of them. If a disabled child was born into a family, the doctor gave the child a lethal injection.

"Now children, you understand how lucky we are to be born in our country? In the Soviet Union, we do not kill our disabled children. The state teaches you, provides you with medical treatment, and feeds you for free. You have to study hard so you can acquire a useful profession."

I don't want them to feed me for free, and I can never have a useful profession. All I want is the injection, the lethal injection. I want to go to America.

Retard

I am a retard. That's not an insult, just a statement of fact. If I can't walk, the medical books say that I am too retarded for an independent existence, for basic survival. Ever since I was a child, I've known that there are two ways to be retarded: mildly and severely. Someone mildly retarded is intellectually backward but can live in a society without assistance. As a standard example of mildly retarded people, they usually mention somebody with mental problems who, through teachers and doctors' efforts, could become professional painters or janitors. Teachers taught me how to solve complex equations, and health care workers dosed me assiduously with medicines and solicitously applied hard plaster casts—but their efforts were futile. I am still not strong enough to lift a paintbrush.

——— ◆ ———

One of my first childhood memories is a conversation I overheard between grownups.

"You are saying he is smart. But he can't walk."

Nothing's changed since then. My entire life, people have talked about my disability in terms of the ability or inability to perform mechanical actions: walking, eating, drinking, using the toilet. But the main thing never changed: I couldn't walk. Grownups are hardly interested in anything else. You can't walk, and therefore you are a retard.

Another children's home, another move. They took me to that orphanage from the clinic, where they tried to get me back on my feet for two years—without success. The treatment was simple. They would put my twisted legs in casts, periodically cut the plaster in certain places, press on the joints, and set my legs in a new position. After a year and a half, my legs were straight. They tried to put me on crutches but realized it was pointless and discharged me. During the treatment, my legs hurt all the time, and I couldn't think straight. According to the law, every child of school age in the Soviet Union has a right to an education. Those who could walk went to the classrooms in the clinic. For others, a teacher visits the wards to teach them there. A teacher came to see me a couple of times too, but when she became convinced of my impenetrable obtuseness, she left me in peace. The teachers pitied the poor child and gave me a "satisfactory" in all my subjects. Thus I was promoted from grade to grade.

When they put me in the clinic, I was in second grade; when they discharged me, I went into my fourth. Everything was the way it was supposed to be according to law. They carried me into the classroom and put me on the floor.

A math lesson was in progress. I was in luck. That day the class had been given a test. A math test is a big deal, and for this serious undertaking, the school's pedagogical council had scheduled a double period, two classes, each forty-five minutes long.

The teacher asked me a couple of questions and ascertained that the boy needed to be in a second-grade class, and she has settled down. She summoned an attendant and told her to take me back to the sleeping wing.

The attendant arrived. She took a look at me.

"I just carried him in, and now I have to carry him out? I am not a mule. I have rights, too. And they call themselves educated. And now, just because they didn't figure it out ahead of time, I have to strain myself? If it wasn't for the war, I might have become a teacher too, you know."

The attendant's voice grew louder and louder. The teacher listened carefully and finally gave up. She politely asked the attendant to leave and apologized for disturbing her. The attendant left, and we could start the test.

The teacher quickly wrote the problems on the board. When she finished, she sat down.

I looked at the board, but I didn't understand anything. Instead of numbers, the problems had letters. I knew perfectly well what plus and minus where—before I came to the clinic, I have been the best student of all—but the multiplication signs looked like simple errors.

"There is a mistake in the examples,"—I blurted out. "Why do you write letters instead of numbers? You can't add letters."

"That's not a mistake. Those letters represent numbers. The goal is to find out which numbers the letters represent. That is called solving an equation."

"You mean if one plus X equals three, then X is two? That's like a brainteaser in a magazine."

"That's right, more or less."

"Then why is X written between two numbers in the second example?"

"That's not the letter X. It's a multiplication sign. You can write it either as a dot or as a small letter x. I wrote an x on the board so that people in the back rows can see it better."

I didn't know what multiplication was. For some reason, the doctors in the hospital were more worried about how much two times two is, and three times three than anything in the world. If I gave the wrong answer, they laughed loudly and told me the right one, and sometimes gave me a piece of candy or a cookie. If they'd explained right away that multiplication is consecutive addition, that wouldn't have made things any easier for me. My legs hurt so badly, and I didn't like the doctors.

The teacher explained multiplication to me.

"Why am I explaining all of this to you?" the teacher continued. You don't even know your multiplication tables."

"Yes, I do, but only to five. I also remember that six times six is thirty-six."

"And seven times eight?"

"Just a sec."

I started adding the numbers out loud. I gave her the correct answer.

"Smart boy!" the teacher praised me.

"It's easy," I said. "When you explain it, everything is easy. Tell me some more."

"You wouldn't understand."

"Yes, I would. You just said yourself I was a smart boy."

The teacher walked briskly to the board and wrote the lesson. She writes and writes. From time to time, she stopped and asked me, "Understand?". I understood everything. She told me about mathematics, and I kept interrupting her questions. Go on, I begged her, go on. We were smiling at each other. It was all so easy.

"That's it. That's everything. I have told you everything you should know as of today as a fourth-grade student."

"Can I take the test?"

"I am not sure you'll pass, but you can give it a try."

I tried.

The hour and a half passed very quickly, and the class handed in their tests. The teacher leaned down, took the sheet of paper from me, and looked over it quickly. Then she looked at me. Her eyes were cold and alien—not like just before, at the board. I understood everything.

It's not all that hard to be a retard. Everyone looks right past you. They ignore you. You are not a person; you are nothing. But sometimes, out of natural kindness or due to professional necessity, the person I am talking to finds out that inside you are the same as everyone else. In an instant, indifference is replaced by delight, then the delight by dull despair in the face of reality.

I didn't look at the teacher. They are all the same. I was sure that at that moment, she is thinking about the same thing as everyone else in her place—about my legs. The legs are the main thing, and math is just nonsense, entertainment.

Sasha

We had known each other since we were five. He used to bully me. Then we became friends. His mother often treated me to candies, and once she gave me a wind-up toy. A commanding, strong, and very good woman, she had raised a fine son. Only recently—about five years ago—I learned that she'd wanted to adopt me. They wouldn't let her. When I, a grown man by then, asked her why she wanted me. She understood perfectly and answered simply:

"Sasha wouldn't have been so bored. You could have played together. You could have gone to college because you are smart, not like my dunce. I would have made a professor out of you."

I looked into the eyes of this smart Russian woman and believed that if they'd let her, she'd have knocked down every wall, gone through every trial, carried me in her arms to the lecture halls, but she would have made a mathematics professor out of this black-eyed Spanish boy. Neither a doctor nor a teacher, she discerned in the eyes of a five-year-old boy what so many medical commissions would attempt and fail to find. I know she wouldn't have bothered to read the diagnoses of my "retarded brain activity" or "mental debility." She had seen my eyes.

I am going to write about her son Sasha, though. A boy who had a mama.

———— ◆ ————

I can barely remember that distant childhood when we were tots. I only really got to know Sasha when fate brought us together in another of my children's homes.

He would crawl down the hall singing:

Into the ring the strongman came

A single shrug and he snapped his chain

Sasha was very different from us. His mom held a high-ranked position in the Soviet retail system, and she raised him simply. She took him to work with her and showed him the practical side of life. He knew about accounts and bills, how goods in short supply got distributed, and why they gave us so little hot cereal for breakfast.

He would crawl down the hall singing. He had a loud voice that could be heard far away. He greeted the attendants and teachers he met loudly. He called them "staff." He'd been sent to school late. That is why he was much older than his classmates. His mama had put a lot of time and effort into trying to cure him. Like all mamas, she wanted to see her son healthy and happy.

I was stunned by his loud singing. I didn't like the way he talked to the attendants. Too often, he was deliberately rude to them. "Hey, Manya, don't be a Scrooge. Give me a little more cereal. And give some to this dude, too. Do you think that if he has no parents and there is no one to stand for him, then there is no need to feed him at all?" At the time, I didn't realize that he was using this intentional rudeness to conceal his shyness. For me, the nannies were demigods, but when it came to crudeness and swearing, he could respond in kind.

At the time, I didn't understand anything.

———— ◆ ————

Sasha has received a package. His mom realized that life in a children's home wasn't all milk and honey, so she sent him a lot of food. As a loving mother, she wanted Sasha to go to school and have friends. That is why she brought him to the children's home in the first place. She took him home for all school vacations and in the summer. And she made his life at the children's home as pleasant as she could by sending packages and leaving him money.

There were different kinds of mothers. The stupid ones brought and sent their children candy. The smart mothers brought them lard, garlic, and home canning—regular food.

Sasha's mom wasn't just a smart one; she was also a big boss. She would send fancy packages with chocolate and canned meat, canned pineapple, and avocado juice. That day he received two boxes at once, each weighing eleven kilos. Sasha was particularly proud of that weight.

"According to Soviet postal regulations, private individuals are allowed packages weighing ten kilos, but "—and here he paused—"in special cases, they accept packages up to eleven kilos."

We didn't understand anything about postal regulations then, but we shared Sasha's joy in full. The bigger the packages, the better. That was obvious.

A teacher aide brought him the two packages, grunting and cursing all doting parents.

"Sasha, according to the children's home rules, I can't give you more than two hundred grams of food at one time. Your ration is balanced, and it's bad for you to overeat. I have to check its quality in advance."

She shouldn't have said that.

"And you are going to check this with a special instrument or, excuse me, by tasting? I don't see any instrument. So, let's make a deal. You check a can of meat and a can of pineapple, leave me the rest, and then we go our separate ways. Okay?"

"How could you think such a thing? I don't need your meat. Take what you like, and I will put your packages away."

"Then let's do this. I am not going to choose anything right now, and you put the packages away. Tomorrow you can bring them back, and then I won't take anything either. You are required to bring me these packages. And you'll bring them to me every day—for a couple of months until my mom comes to visit. And then you'll explain to my mother about overeating and food quality. Believe me, she is in trade, and she knows everything about food quality."

The teacher aide wasn't exactly thrilled by the prospect of a chat with Sasha's mother.

Sasha was a clever boy. He understood that you have to leave your opponent a way out.

"Here is an idea! For now, you just check all the expiration dates on the cans and boxes and take out the ones that have expired. And don't worry about the two hundred grams. I am not going to eat the food alone or in one night."

The teacher aide was pleased with this turn of events. No one wanted to quarrel with Sasha's mother. Not only that, but she realized his mother wasn't going to send her son just anything. She conscientiously checked all the foods—so there wouldn't be any that had expired. Sasha could keep his packages, and he, with a lordly gesture, offered the teacher aide a can of meat. The teacher aide refused. The Sasha took a can of pineapple out of the box.

"You have children. Please give this to them."

The teacher aide hesitated. She would have liked to bring her children the pineapple, but she was still angry at Sasha, at his way of talking to her, a representative of authority and an adult. "For the children, for the children"—Sasha repeated and looked her in the eye.

Suddenly the aide smiled, took the pineapple, and left. She was a good woman and realized that Sasha wasn't ridiculing her.

The Soviet Union is a country of universal shortages. Shortages are when something isn't for sale and can't be bought at any price. The workers at the children's home often came to Sasha, asking him to "obtain" something they couldn't. Usually, Sasha refused. He didn't want to play these grown-up games. He wasn't mean or greedy, but he knew that his mom was in no position to supply everyone with the things they couldn't get. The teacher aide asked him to "obtain" buckwheat groats. There was a shortage of buckwheat. Her mom had diabetes, and she needed buckwheat. Her mom couldn't eat anything, or rather, she required a strict diet. Buckwheat was one of the meals she was allowed. Sasha wrote his mom a letter, and she sent the buckwheat groats.

The teacher aide brought Sasha the package. In it were two kilos of groats. She looked at Sasha. And waited.

"Buckwheat groats, top quality," said Sasha, "price, forty-eight kopeks a kilo. Here are two kilos. That will be ninety-six kopeks."

"Fine, Sasha. I'll write down that you have ninety-six kopeks."

The problem was that at children's home, the children were not allowed to have cash.

Stupid moms and dads would give the money to the teacher aide. The child could ask the teacher aide for something, and the next day the person on duty would bring his order. That was how you could buy candies or a pencil, for example. But a teacher aide could not be asked to purchase anything forbidden. Not only wine and cigarettes, but canned fish, eggs, pastries, and homemade foods were not allowed. There is no need to explain how much we valued cash.

"No. That won't work." Sasha said. "This isn't business. You already have my fifty rubles there. You won't give me the ninety-six kopeks?"

"No. It's forbidden. And what are you going to do with raw groats anyway?"

"I'll sell them to Dusya. She is an attendant, and she couldn't care less about what you forbid."

"But I need the buckwheat for my mom. You promised."

"I don't have anything against your mom. Let her eat buckwheat with pleasure. But I promised to sell you the buckwheat, not give it up for free."

"Fine. Take a rouble, and we're even."

"No. You owe me exactly ninety-six kopeks. I don't have four kopeks."

The teacher aide decided to play along. She went for a change.

The deal went through.

For breakfast, they've given us buckwheat hot cereal. Buckwheat groats are a rarity in the children's home. They've given us two spoonfuls of buckwheat hot cereal apiece, and we are happy. Only Sasha isn't. He is cursing, and the veins on his neck are bulging. He slings a curt "swine," takes his portion of hot cereal from the table, and crawls to the room where the attendants are eating.

Sasha has a healthy upper body. His legs are twisted into an unimaginable pretzel, and one arm is paralyzed. He crawls towards the attendants' room, opens the door with his head, and hurls the plate of buckwheat into the room with his healthy arm.

Sitting at the table at the attendants' room is an attendant with her daughter and husband. In front of each is a full plate of buckwheat.

The man lifts his head from the plate. He sees Sasha and hears what he's saying. Sasha is ranting about how the attendant is not only getting fat on someone else's misery but is also feeding her fat-faced daughter and her fancy man. Naturally, Sasha doesn't use exactly those words. He expresses himself in normal Russian, spiced with some choice curses. I won't try to repeat what he says. The man drops his spoons full of buckwheat, and all he says is: "Manya, let's have a word." Sasha crawls away from the door, and they go out.

Manya returns with a black eye and a full bucket of hot buckwheat cereal. They'd been plenty in the dining room, and she's just been too lazy to carry out the whole bucket.

Sasha was accused of smoking. He always had money, so he could even have bought expensive cigarettes. But he didn't smoke. He did not smoke in principle.

That day, he stocked up on cigarettes, crawled to the teachers' room door, and lit up. He smoked intently, inhaling deeply. The teachers walked up and looked at the impudent boy, but didn't do anything about it. Cigarette smoke filled the hallway and was already filtering into the teachers' room. Finally, the school's director came.

We had a very good director.

He squatted in front of Sasha.

"Put out the cigarette."

Sasha did.

"Finally. I thought I was going to have to smoke it all?"

"What are you smoking?"

"Kosmos. Filthy stuff, of course, but at least it has a filter."

"Why were you smoking outside the teachers' room?"

"I was waiting for you."

"Why? You know smoking is bad for your health. Even filtered cigarettes."

"I don't smoke. Do you think I am fool enough to poison myself and pay money to do it on top of that? It's just that they accused me of smoking. I don't care, but the teacher aide is sure that I am sneaking around. If I decide to smoke, I will smoke out in the open. My health is my own business. But I won't let anyone accuse me of sneaking around. If she wants to smoke so badly, I will smoke right in front of her."

"You mean you were so insulted by her lack of trust, so you decided to protest right here?"

"Yes."

"Fine, I will have a word with her. Do you have any cigarettes left?"

"Two and a half packs."

"Will you give them to me?"

"There are pretty expensive cigarettes."

The director smiled and fumbled in his pocket for money. He took the cigarettes away, gave Sasha the money, and walked into the teachers' room.

That children's home had a very good director.

———— ❖ ————

We had great teachers—the people who are inspired by their profession. Of course, the teachers have a job that was much easier than the one of the attendants. They didn't have to take care of us. For me, a teacher's opinion meant nothing compared to an attendant's. Nevertheless, teachers remained adults, useful for society, and I was a useless piece of meat. Sasha didn't think so.

One day, a new teacher of the Russian language came to their class. The people who stumbled into this job were weeded out quickly, and nothing helped, not even substantial hardship bonuses. This one was substituting for a teacher who has taken ill.

Dictation. All the students are sitting at their benches. Sasha is lying on the floor. Leaning on his bad arm and assiduously making large, ugly letters with this good one. Spasms wrack his body, but he is making an honest effort.

"Excuse me, but could you dictate slower?"

"I am dictating at the appropriate speed for sixth grade." Sasha smiles.

"You see, if I had hands of a sixth-grade student, I wouldn't be bothering you."

"In that case, you should study in a special ed school."

Sasha doesn't take offense. He puts down his pen and reaches into his schoolbag for a book.

"What do you think you are doing?"

"Reading. I won't be able to write, and we're not allowed to bother the others doing an assignment."

"Stop this instant."

"Will you dictate slower?"

Her patience snaps. The boy is nothing but a smart aleck. He could have just asked. In his situation, he can't be choosy, can he? He has to be punished. She spends a long time writing something in the classroom record.

"I am going to call your parents in."

"From Leningrad? Mom won't come. At most, she will call the director." "Fine. Then I won't let you go to independent study, and you will get a' poor' in all your subjects."

That at she has evening duty.

The teacher is walking behind the attendants. The three sturdy women put Sasha in a wheelchair and try to take him back to the sleeping wing. He turns to the teacher:

"Why don't you take me back? Are you afraid to overexert yourself?"

And to the attendants:

"All right, girls, you have no choice, let's go."

He grabs one wheel of the chair with his good hand. Spasms wrack his body, and it hurts a lot, but there is virtually no way to detach his hand from the wheel's spokes. The attendants have to drag the chair with the locked wheel. They curse the teacher at the top of their lungs, but they drag the chair cursing softly at Sasha.

And Sasha sings. He sings about a Russian ship that refused to surrender to the enemy's superior forces.

Our Varangian, proud shall never yield.

And no man asks for mercy

He's carted off to the sleeping wing and unloaded onto the floor. The teacher is happy. Sasha's' poor' grades are a sure thing tomorrow.

That evening, after the children have eaten and the children's home workers are just sitting down to have their supper, Sasha crawls over to the school.

It's winter. It's snowing. It's late.

The school isn't far, a few hundred meters. Sasha uses his good arm to rake the snow under him and cautiously shifts his bad arm. The worst part of it all is that the snow has melted just a little, and his bad arm keeps slipping on the icy asphalt, so he can't crawl very fast.

He is dressed like all us non-walkers. Leggings and a shirt, which is unbuttoned. He is not showing off, it's just that the shirt keeps slipping down one shoulder and the buttons have come undone.

He crawls into the school building and then into his classroom and reads the textbooks for the next day.

The attendants discover the child is missing, follow his trail, and call for the teacher.

"Come and deal with him yourself."

She walks into the room and takes a look at Sasha.

"What are you doing here?"

"I am exercising my constitutional right. I am doing my homework."

"But why did you crawl through the snow?"

"I didn't have any choice. I had to show you that you can't conquer me with brute force. Yes, and arrange some transportation because I am not going to crawl back."

The teacher runs out. Later they told us she became hysterical and cried for a long time, but we didn't believe it. We didn't think that teachers could cry over something that unimportant.

——— ◆ ———

A few years later, I pay Sasha a visit.

"Mom, bring the vodka. Ruben and I are going to have a drink."

"But, you didn't even drink at New Year's."

"New Year's comes every year, but I haven't seen Ruben for six."

We drink vodka and talk, and I ask him a crucial question.

"Sasha, are you glad the children's home was part of your life?"

"No. After the children's home, I changed. I wish I'd never known it."

"But you had friends in the children's home. You met me."

Sasha thinks about this.

"Forgive me, Ruben. You are a fine fellow and my friend, and I am glad I met you. But I wish there'd never been a children's home."

New York

The classroom supervisor is giving us political instruction again. We are being told about the horrors of the Western way of life. We're used to this, so nothing surprises us. I am absolutely convinced that most people in America live in cardboard boxes. I was sure that every American is building a bomb shelter, and the country is experiencing one crisis after another.

That time they're telling us about New York City. They cite an article from the New York Times about free cheese being distributed to the unemployed. Several tons were handed out, one hundred grams per person. The teacher puts particular emphasis on the fact these poor folks won't get anything next month. I ask whether they won't starve to death then.

"Of course they will," the teacher replies. "But new crowds of fired workers will come to take their place." I believe her.

◆

We are alone in the classroom, the history teacher and me. He is writing something in the classroom record, and I am reading. He is sitting at the teacher's desk, and I am lying on the floor nearby.

"Are you very busy?"

"What do you want?"

He looks up from his work. The teacher has very kind and intelligent eyes and slightly graying hair. There is a pin on his jacket lapel.

"I have a question."

"Ask away."

"In political class, they told us that people in capitalist countries live in terrible poverty on the brink of starving to death. I was doing some figuring here, and everything adds up. They have billionaires in America, but very few. Right?"

"Right."

"They have millionaires too. Not many, but still lots more than billionaires. And there have to be many times more people of moderate means—shopkeepers and hairdressers—than there are millionaires. And many times more workers than shopkeepers. And many times more unemployed than workers. Right?"

"Right. That's no surprise. People there live very badly."

"You agree? Then according to my rough estimate, several hundred thousand unemployed people must be dying on the streets of New York, for instance, because they have nothing to eat. And that's not counting the workers starving to death. New York City must be piled high with corpses. Someone has to keep clearing them out. I don't understand these Americans. Walking down the streets surrounded by people who are starving or starved to death. Why haven't they thrown out their landowners and capitalists yet?"

The teacher stands up, walks over, and squats in front of me. He gives me a strange look and smiles. He is almost laughing at my serious problem. He probably just in a very good mood today.

"How old are you?"

"You know, I am ten."

"I know, I know," he says, now very cheerfully. "Isn't it a little early for you to be worrying about these things?"

I don't answer.

"Don't be angry. It's just a little too complicated for you."

The teacher stands up, takes the classroom record from the desk, and walks toward the door, where turns around and gives me a serious, stern look as if seeing for the first time.

"Not a soul, you hear? Don't bring this topic up with anyone. You are a big boy now, you should understand."

The next day he comes over to me, bends down, and puts a big handsome book on the floor.

"Read this. It's a serious historical novel. I know you'll like it."

The Cutlet

I was an obedient student. I always listen to adults. At the end of every school year, I was solemnly awarded an honorary certificate "for an excellent study and exemplary behavior." It is true, I was an excellent student, and the term "exemplary behavior" meant I never argued with my teachers. It was easy to get along with the teachers; they were always going on about utter nonsense. They spent hours telling us absolutely unnecessary and pointless things we were supposed to recite. I have a good memory, and I had no trouble regurgitating the lessons. The teachers thought I was trying very hard. Strange people. I liked going to school, where everything was for fun. They gave us books with beautiful pictures and notebooks that were either ruled or squared. The school was like a game. I played with pleasure.

But I had to obey all adults. The hardest part was obeying the attendants. They didn't care what the smart books with pretty pictures say. A Pushkin poem learned by heart or a mathematical formula didn't change anything. They demanded only one thing of me: that I ask for as little help as possible. Starting from about five years old, they started telling me that I am too heavy because I am eating too much. "You keep gobbling away, and we have to carry you. You have no conscience. They gave birth to a Negro, and now we have to lug him around his whole life. We do not care. We are just stupid Russian women. We are too kind, so we are putting up with this. We are taking care of him. But his parents are clever. They ran off to their home in Africa." And so it was, from one day to the next. I had to listen to them every day talking about their kindness and compassion, and my black-skinned parents. It's a little funny, but I had to hear this same text in every institution in the Soviet Union—children's homes, hospitals, old folks' homes. It was as if they were reading from the same secret script, like a textbook or a spell.

I tried the best I could. But the best I could do was to eat and drink less. I didn't know how to live without eating at all, and there was no one around to ask. It didn't make sense to ask the teachers because they were not the real thing. They didn't have to bring the bedpans to us. I learned from the attendants that the teachers' job was much easier, but their pay was much higher. From the attendants' perspective, the teachers were being paid for doing nothing, and I fully agreed with the attendants. It's easy to tell stories from pretty books. Taking out the bedpans is hard work. That I understood very well.

But there was occasionally some use to be had from the teachers. Good teachers would bring books and magazines from home. In one ladies' magazine, I read about dieting. If you don't want to get fat, you have to cut meat and starch from your daily ration. I stopped eating bread and macaroni. They did not spoil us meat products often, but occasionally they gave us cutlets[1]. It was hard to deny oneself cutlets, but I did, with the help of a smart book about secret agents. The book said that a real man has to exercise his willpower every day. So I did. At first, I got really hungry, but then I got used to it. When they'd bring us our meal, I would automatically pick out what I allowed myself to eat. Usually, I limited myself to stewed fruit and a couple of spoonfuls of hot cereal. My mood improved. Now I was doing everything right except that I was always sleepy, and by the third period in school, I couldn't think straight, and I felt dizzy. I fainted a few times in class.

One day my stomach started to hurt, and I didn't make it to the toilet on time. The attendant carried me there, put me on the floor, and started lecturing me. She yelled at me, told me how bad I was, and went on and on about the "black-assed bitch" and how they all took such good care of me and how I was so ungrateful. I didn't say anything. What was there to say? That wasn't the first time this happened. It didn't make sense to cry and ask for her compassion because all my words fell apart against the sole argument—my soiled pants. She was yelling harder and harder, leaning over me, shaking her jowly cheeks, spraying spittle. I didn't say anything. What could I say? She was right. I was too fat and thought about food all the time. I was nearly eleven, and I already weighed almost seventeen kilos. I couldn't justify myself. I hated myself, too, for my weakness. Two days ago, I had a whole cutlet. I was not hungry, honestly. I thought I'd just smell it, and then I took a bite. Before I knew it, I ate the whole thing.

I didn't say anything. Then she grabbed my head with her greasy fingers and started jamming my face to my dirty pants.

"Look at him, all silent! Say something! Beg for forgiveness, promise that you won't be doing that again. Say anything!"

---

[1] Cutlet or Côtelette traditionally is a thin slice of meat from the ribs of veal, pork, or chicken, often breaded. In Russian cuisine, cutlets are meat patties.

She was jamming my nose into my shit and repeating very softly: "Say it, say it, say it." What could I say? I knew perfectly well that what they wanted from me had nothing to do with words. I already tried the words. The attendant wants, really wants only one thing: for me to learn to go to the toilet by myself. That was a promise I couldn't make, and therefore I didn't say anything.

"Say it, say it, say it! Are you going to say it? Are you?" she kept repeating in a monotone. "Say it, say it!" It was like in a film about the war where the German officer interrogated a brave Russian partisan. A German officer. A German.

All of a sudden, a simple German sentence came out of me: "Russisches Schwein."

"Du bist Russische Schwein," I shouted in a desperate rage. "Du bist ein Russisches Schwein. Russisches Schwein. Russisches Schwein. Russisches Schwein." The German were right to shoot your parents. "They should have shot you too."

It was words, nothing but words. But they were effective. The woman lost it. As a child, she had lived through the German occupation and the postwar famine. I knew I was hitting her where it hurt.

I am used to my disability. Only occasionally, just for a minute, I suddenly have an irresistible desire to stand up on my feet. This desire usually emerges spontaneously, from somewhere in the depths of my animal core. I had a powerful urge to pick up a sharp knife with my right hand and thrust it into her fat belly. To hit her again and again. To disembowel her. I wanted revenge.

I began to cry. I was crying and screaming. I was shouting unfair and awful things into the face of this stupid woman. I was shouting obscenities and trying to hurt her as severely as I could.

A teacher was walking by. She came in at my shouting and saw my lying naked on the cement floor in shit and tears. She understood immediately and raised a hue and cry. Kind adults washed me and carried me to my bed. The nurse came with a syringe.

"Calm down, little boy. Everything is going to be all right. I am going to give you a nice shot now, and you'll fall asleep."

"Get away from me, you bitch, you slut! You are Russian! I hate you! I hate all Russians! Nazi, swine. A nice little shot? Yes, give me the shot. But not that one. I need a real one, to die for good. I am black-ass, and you are Russians. Kill me now and stop torturing me. You won't even waste your poison on me. You are worse than the Nazis. The Nazis killed all the disabled people, but you are excruciating me."

They gave me a shot. I am yelling. I told them everything: about the diet, about being fat. I promised them I wouldn't eat anything anymore. The teachers and nurse listened to me but didn't understand. They tried to calm me down.

The shot worked. I fell asleep quickly and slept through to midday. I felt better. Calm. At dinner, they gave me a cutlet. I decided to eat everything. I ate the cutlet, the borscht, and the bread. So what, if I got fat? I didn't care anymore.

The German

He came into our classroom with a quick, mincing step, pulled out a chair, and sat down. Without looking at us, he began reciting poetry, loudly and clearly. He recited for a long time, then stood up and surveyed the class. "That was Goethe. I was reciting in German. Maybe one day, you will be able to read Goethe in the original. I am your new foreign language teacher."

He walked over to the desk and opened the textbook. "First of all, I must apologize to Ruben. Ruben, I am very sorry I can't teach you Spanish. I don't know Spanish. Study German for now. If you learn German, you can learn any other language. Remember that." I did.

It was a strange teacher, peculiar. Every once in a while, he would get carried away in the middle of a lesson and recite poetry for a long time. He told us about Germany with passion and excitement. He radiated with joy when a German soccer team won a match. He considered everything German the best. A real teacher—a weirdo and a fanatic.

———— ◆ ————

The German lesson. Our class is all worked up, and we are arguing with the teacher. The topic of our argument—Germany's superiority—never changed. You could ask him anything except Germany's defeat in the Second World War. If you mentioned the war, the teacher got quiet and started wiping his glasses. Then, in a dry, colorless voice, he will tell us to open the textbooks on the specified page and recite those endless German verbs.

His eyes are burning, and his cheeks are flushed. He is triumphantly tossing out to the class the names of German composers, philosophers, and poets. He is practically shouting about the superiority of German shipwrights. He is happy, pleased. There is nothing we can say. We move on to a discussion of agriculture. We listen ecstatically to what he says about bushels and hectares, about production volumes and incredible harvests.

Someone's timid question spoils everything:

"What about dates?"

"What dates?"

"Do they grow dates in Germany?"

He droops. His mood is ruined. We recite those endless German verbs.

--- ◆ ---

He comes over to me and sits down. He is holding a little paper bag full of dates.

"Want some?"

"Thank you."

We eat the dates in silence. We ate them all. He rises heavily from the floor, brushed off his pants, and sighs.

"But dates don't grow in Germany. That's the truth. They don't grow there at all."

Music

The music records weren't ours. It was someone else's. The music had been recorded on "ribs[1]." The children's home residents brought in blank X-ray films from their endless trips to hospitals, then exchanged them for the embossed ones at a rate of one to two. It was a business.

The innocuous Western hits terrified our teachers.

"Do you understand what they are singing about?"

We didn't. The records were taken away. The violators' behavior was discussed at the school's pedagogical council; the fight against capitalist influence was in full swing. A pointless fight.

The boys started wearing their hair long. Instructions were sent from Moscow on how to fight this "contagion". The students' hair was not supposed to fall below mid-ear. Ears were measured with a ruler, and their midpoints were gauged by eye. There was an eternal struggle to wear your hair a little bit snazzier than your friend's.

The arguments over long hair didn't concern me. They always shaved my head because I wasn't a walking one.

I really want to know what people sing about on the records. I want to learn their language.

---

[1] Used X-rays films are made of plastic, so one can use it instead of vinyl to record music that can be played on the turntable.

The Letter

It was a bad children's home, just a horrible. The food was terrible, and the adults were nasty. Everything was bad. Orphanages, like prisons, are different. This one was particularly bad. The hardest thing was to endure the cold. The building was not heated. That was particularly hard in winter. The ink froze in our pens. It was freezing in the classrooms and cold in the sleeping wing—no matter where I crawled, it was cold. In other children's homes, it was only cold in the hallways, but in this one, it was cold everywhere. In other children's homes, you could crawl over to the radiator, but this one had nothing but useless pieces of cold metal inside. It was a bad children's home, just a terrible.

They brought in a new kid. Cerebral palsy. The boy was large and strong, and he writhed with constant violent spasms. Spasms like that are rare. The attendants took him by the arm and put him on his bed.

His face was contorted, and his speech unintelligible, or nearly unintelligible. I understood everything. He was not very smart, but also not a complete imbecile, as almost everyone assumed, from teachers to peers. He sat on his bed, continuously repeating a strange sound—a birdlike screech, klsk, klsk—like an incantation. There are no words in Russian made up entirely of consonants. I knew that and read the vowels on his lips, or rather from his facial muscles' movement. The boy wasn't crazy. Day and night, he was repeating a simple word: kolyaska (a wheelchair). It was also difficult to call him normal. He did not get it yet. What wheelchair? There is no food here, so there certainly weren't any wheelchairs.

The children in the orphanage had the right to correspond with their parents. Every week the teacher aide urged the children to write letters. And every week, the children stubbornly refused to write home. Those children were so stupid. They were given a free envelope and a free blank sheet of paper.

In the younger grades, nearly everyone wrote letters. The pages with childish scrawl were handed to the teacher aide, who corrected their grammatical errors, put the letters into the envelopes, and mailed them.

Everyone understood exactly what you were supposed to write in letters. Everyone wrote about their grades, the caring adults, their friendly classmates. Every holiday the children were given pretty cards, all identical for sending greetings to their parents. The adults especially liked the cards. Every card had to be ruled off in pencil, and then a draft was written of the greeting text. The teacher aide would correct the mistakes in the draft. Then you could rewrite the text into the card with a pencil and after that, if it had been written without errors, write over the pencil with colored ink. Everyone knew what they couldn't write. You couldn't write about anything bad. For instance, you weren't allowed to write about food. Particularly the food. But in their own letters, the stupid parents, for some reason, always explicitly asked about the food. Therefore, all the letters frequently began with the standard "Dear Mommy. They are feeding us well." The children were praised for good notes and yelled at for bad ones. The particularly bad letters were read out loud to the entire class.

The high-schoolers didn't write letters. Their parents were well aware of what a children's home was. Why cause them unnecessary worry? And if someone did have to write a letter, he could always buy an envelope, assuming he had the money. It was only the dull children who gave their letters to the teacher aide. Everyone knew that according to regulations, she was supposed to take the letter home, read it, and only then decide whether to send it or not. But any adult could drop a letter in the mailbox. Usually, the children asked the attendants for this simple favor, but one boy took advantage of the bread truck drivers. The bread was brought to the children's home every day. He would approach the driver and whisper: "Please drop this letter in the mailbox." The driver would look around, take the letter without saying a word, and get into his truck. This boy's letters were sent this very day; his parents knew it from the postmark. The boy tried proudly to convince us that all truck drivers were good people. His dad was a truck driver.

Maybe the teacher aide really believed that high school students did not write letters. Or, she might have suspected something when, once a week, she urged everyone to write. She would talk, and no one would say a word. That was the drill. If the teacher aide put too much pressure on some of the students, the fellow would have to pretend he'd decided to write a letter. He would write quickly on the sheet of paper, "The pearl barley is fucking fantastic," slip the page in the envelope and seal the envelope with glue we used to make airplane models. Not a single such letter ever reached its intended recipient—not that it needed to. On the other hand, no one bothered the author of the letter again.

The new kid sat on his bed all the time, shouting and crying. At first, the attendants treated him all right. In the morning, they took him off his bed, put him on the floor, and asked him if he is comfortable to start crawling. The disabled boy lay on his back, his arms and legs jerking in the air, and bellowed something incomprehensible. When they turned him over on his stomach, he shouted even harder. The attendants put him back on his bed and left. What else could they do?

He shouted and bellowed and cried. He cried day and night. At first, his classmates felt like beating him up to shut him up, but they didn't. Retards didn't get beaten up. The guys just asked the administration to move him to a different ward. No one wanted to fall asleep to the sound of nocturnal shouting. While the adults were trying to figure out where to put this unfortunate boy, the guys tried to entertain the little the fool. They brought him balls and children's toys, but nothing helped. The guys refused to give up. He had to like something. Someone offered him a notebook, a fat notebook with grid-line papers. The little fool was overjoyed and nodded. He grabbed the notebook, calmed down, and suddenly said clearly: "Give." His unexpected success cheered everyone up. They asked him to say "give" over and over. He would repeat it and smile. The word "give" came well out of him. He could pronounce the words "mama," "papa," "give," and "yes" clearly and almost fluently. He had trouble with "no". It started with an almost inaudible "n", followed by a pause and then a long "o-o-o". But that was enough. He asked for a pen. They gave him a pen and, without him asking, a table that they moved close to his bed. They put the pen on the table. He froze for a moment, picked up the pen with his surprisingly deft right hand, stretched out confidently across the table, holding the notebook steadily beneath him, opened the notebook with his chin, and jabbed the pen at the blank page. He sat up: his outflung arms twitched pointlessly, and his legs under the table beat an arrhythmic tempo. He laughed, and the guys laughed with him.

The new kid's life changed. He slept soundly at night, and in the morning, an attendant stuck a pen in his hand and put the notebook in front of him. He sat on the bed all day, falling on the notebook with his whole body, trying over and over to jab the pen into the blank page, then straightening up, laughing joyfully, admiring his drawings. For two weeks, the guys in the ward slept peacefully. For two weeks, the little fool patiently scratched his bizarre squiggles and purposeful designs—

shapes and signs he alone could make out—in the notebook. When there was no blank space left in the notebook, he yells. Then he yells again. Notebooks were prized in the children's home, especially grid-ruled ones. But the little fool wanted to draw, and the guys wanted to sleep at night. They bought him a new one. Let him draw. He didn't even look at the fresh notebook. He threw the pen on the floor, placed the old notebook—a crumpled, useless toy, next to him on the bed, and started yelling.

Now everyone understood what he was yelling about. He was screaming: "Mama." He was crying loudly. By now, the guys were somewhat used to his way of talking. Everyone tried to get out of him what he needs, to convince him to stop shouting. They promised to bring him many more notebooks, but nothing helped. They said one word after another to him, to each of which he said "no". Then they started naming letters. They were just running through the alphabet, and if he liked the letter, he'd say "yes". What formed was the word "send". That cleared things up. He wanted his drawings sent to his mama. They called the teacher aide, and she examined the notebook for a long time. The crumpled pages were covered solid with symbols of some kind. These symbols would be random in one place and in another clustered thickly into an indistinguishable clump of inky interweavings. Some pages were covered with solid circles. The circles were of different sizes and were not always closed. Only at a stretch would you take them for a letter O. But who would draw the letter O for two pages in a row?

The teacher aide refused to send the notebook to his parents. It's a letter, she said, and I have to know it's content. A scandal was brewing. What content could there be in his clumsy scrawls? The strict teacher got to go home after her shift and get a good night's sleep, while the guys were again being kept awake by this little fool's shouts. How fair was that? The teacher aide had to find a solution to their troubles right away. She went over to the new kid:

"Is this a letter?"

"No."

"Are these your drawings?"

"Yes."

"Do you want me to send them to your mama?"

"Yes."

"What if we don't send your mama the whole notebook? What if we chose the prettiest drawings and sent them?"

"No. No."

He said "no"—a word that was very hard for him—twice. Then he started yelling. He cried: "Mama," stamped his feet and tried to say "no" once more. He couldn't.

"Fine, fine. I understand everything. Your mama likes it a lot when you draw. I will send her all your drawings. I will write a letter to your mama. I will tell her that you like it here very much, you have many friends, and you love to draw. You do like it here with us, don't you?"

"Yes."

So they had their talk. The teacher aide sent the new kid's notebook to his parents. The new kid calmed down. He slept at night and sat on his bed during the day, staring into space.

A month later, they brought wheelchairs to the children's home. There were a lot of wheelchairs. Enough for everyone. They gave the new kid a wheelchair, too. The attendants picked him up under the arms, and he stood up. They led him to the wheelchair, and he sat down. They tried to put his feet on the rests, but he wouldn't let them. They took the footrests off. He pushed off with his feet, and he was on his way. He picked up speed very quickly with his strong legs and rolled down the hallway.

At the next class meeting, the teacher aide yelled at the new kid. She said the same foolish things she usually said in these cases.

How the country was bending over backward to provide us its last crust of bread and how ungrateful he was. She tried to argue that she had treated the new kid like a human being and sent his parents his notebook. And in the notebook, it turns out, he had slung mud over the entire collective and painted life in the home in the blackest colors and found fault with the pedagogical council and the staff for no reason at all. She went on and on and on. The new kid wasn't listening. When she got as far as typical accusations of callousness and heartlessness, he pushed away from his desk and rolled out into the hallway.

They didn't let him write any more letters. Not that he asked. After class, he would roll up and down the hallway and play with balls for hours. At the dinner, he regularly asked for an extra portion. He had to be spoon-fed, and the attendants didn't want to feed him the extra. They tried to explain all this to him, but in vain. He would follow the attendant in his wheelchair until she gave up. The attendants would go to their room to hide from his pestering. He would sit outside the door and shout. When everyone was exasperated, they would come out of the room and give him another soup or hot cereal plate. Gradually everyone got used to him, and they always gave him seconds so that the pesky invalid would leave them in peace.

When we were alone, I talked to him. Slowly pronouncing each word, he would say a sentence and watch me warily. I would repeat what he'd said. Gradually he began to trust me, and I didn't need to repeat what he'd said anymore. We just talked. I asked what exactly has been in this letter.

"Ruben. I was doing a lot of thinking."

"I know you did a lot of thinking, and you wrote a fine letter. What did you write?"

"MAMA, THEY FEED ME BADLY AND WON'T GIVE ME A CHAIR."

By "chair" he'd meant a wheelchair.

The entire first page of the first letter he'd written in his life had been covered with the letter M. Uppercase and lowercase. He had hoped that at least one letter on the whole page would be understood. Sometimes one letter took up several pages. The thick notebook, ninety-six pages, had been completely filled.

"The first four letters were unnecessary," I tried to argue.

"I thought about it for a long time."

"But the first four letters were unnecessary anyway. You might not have had enough room in the notebook.

He thought about that. Then he smiled broadly and said slowly and very clearly: "Ma-ma."

Pirozhki

A children's home, a home for children. A place where children are prepared for their future, their adult life. In addition to general education subjects, they teach the basics of survival for the complicated world that begins outside the school gate. The boys are trained to understand wiring, use a fret-saw, and assemble and repair furniture. The girls learn to sew, knit, and cook. It's not so easy, teaching a boy without hands to change electrical plugs, and teaching one-armed girl to knit seems almost impossible. It's hard. Indeed, it's very hard. Our teachers were able to accomplish things that parents of a disabled child could not even have imagined.

I am lying on the classroom floor. A girl comes in carrying a tray. She has a prosthetic in place of one leg, but by our children's home standards, she is practically healthy. On the tray are pirozhki. Hot and golden.

"Where are the boys?" she says, "The girls and I, we baked pirozhki, and they promised to stop by the kitchen and try them."

"They went to the movies."

"What do you mean, the movies?"

"They got taken to the movies today. Tomorrow, they will take you. You see, you have a cooking class."

"But why didn't they tell us? What are we supposed to do with the pirozhki now?"

She puts the tray on the teacher's desk, sits down on the bench, takes a pirozhok from the tray, and hands it to me.

A pirozhok with potatoes and onion. I am eating a pirozhok.

"It's delicious," I say, "Your pirozhki came out fine."

The girl doesn't hear me. She is staring off into space.

"That's odd. Where are the boys?"

The Fight

Fights were a rarity in the children's home. When we did fight, though, we fought cruelly. Only scum bit or pulled hair, and knives and brass knuckles were off-limits for us. If the degree of disability was unequal, vengeance was allowed. There were no expiration dates on revenge. I knew a guy who proudly described how he'd pushed off his offender under a car for an insult inflicted a year and a half earlier. He hadn't done a very good job at it, though. The car was just picking up speed, and the boy wasn't hit hard enough. At the evening gathering, the offender was acquitted. He had only one arm, and the boy he had pushed had two arms and a leg. It was all fair and square. A fight would have been impossible. The one-armed boy had taken his revenge—that is, he had acted appropriately. When his victim was discharged from the hospital, the two became friends. The strength was respected. Everyone had the right to be strong.

◆

I loved autumn. In the fall, the ones who were lucky to spend the holiday at home come back. The autumn was noisy and fun, and there were a lot of delicious food and exciting talk about home, the summer, and parents. I always hated spring. I still do. In the spring, my best friend went away for vacation. Every spring, we hoped that someone would be taken home this year who had not been taken last year. Everyone had these hopes—even those parents lived too far away, even the orphans. We would try to spend most of the day in the schoolyard, near the gate. We didn't talk about it; we just waited. We just hoped. I never hoped because I knew that no one would ever come for me.

That autumn, Seryoga has returned unhappy. It was odd seeing a sad Seryoga. Of course, everyone was a little sad after vacation, and everyone missed home. But their sadness was relieved by seeing their friends, by new impressions and new textbooks. We moved up a grade; we were older.

Seryoga, an overgrown legless fellow, came to see us in our ward on his trolley. He wanted to consult with the lads. He spoke mainly with Genka.

"I was called for a fight."

"Seryoga, you are the strongest boy in the home. Everyone knows that. Who would ever fight you?"

"That is the point. That is not in the orphanage, it is out there, on the outside."

"What is the fight about?"

"A woman. They said they'd drive me to my grave, dig me into the ground. The day before I left to come back here. They said if I showed up next spring, they'd killed me."

Everyone knew that Seryoga had a girl waiting for him on the outside. A healthy girl. A normal, pretty girl. Our girls didn't even attempt to flirt with him. They knew that when Seryoga graduated high school, he'd marry his girlfriend.

Genka didn't ask about the woman. That just wasn't done. If the guy wanted to, he'd talk himself. If he didn't, that's his business.

"I don't know what to tell you. I have never been on the outside. Is he strong?"

"Of course. And a year older than me. He goes to junior college."

"Then you're fucked. He will kill you. He'll give you and good kick and trample you to death."

"I know that. But I have to fight."

Genka pondered this. There was no one smarter than Genka in the orphanage. He knew it himself. That is a children's home. Here it is impossible to hide anything. Everyone knew everything about everyone. We knew who was the strongest in the orphanage, in which class has the most beautiful girl.

"You know, Seryoga, I think you have a chance. A small one, but a chance. You have to knock him down. If he falls—throw yourself on top of him and smother him. He is two legs bigger than you, so he is stronger. You don't have any other option."

Seryoga knew he had no other option. From that day on, he started working out. That year everyone was working out. They set up horizontal bars in the schoolyard, and the electrician and phys ed teacher slapped together a few primitive weight benches out of metal pipes. There were a lot fewer drinking parties. The teachers were happy because the children spent nearly all their free time in the schoolyard.

Seryoga, an influential fellow, quit smoking, and so did the others who decided to work out. Later, most of them gave up and started smoking again. But not Seryoga.

Every day. An hour in the morning, two hours in the evening, and four hours each on Saturday and Sunday. For nine months of the school year, the children's home worked out.

Those who were missing an arm worked out the muscles of the one they had. All of a sudden, they started wearing their prosthetics. The formerly useless plastic imitation arms did indeed become essential. Each boy would fill his prosthetic with pig iron, depending on how much training he was doing, so he wouldn't pull his back out or twist his spine favoring his good side. Meanwhile, the prosthetic itself wasn't a wrong weapon in a fight.

There was one armless fellow in the children's home. He didn't have any arms at all. Those who were missing only arms could develop their stumps for fighting with prosthetics. But his prosthetics, useless toys, only got in his way, so he didn't wear them at all. He worked out more than anyone else, even more than Seryoga. He would sit on a stool, hook his feet under a cupboard, and lean back, touching the floor with his head's top. He was always working out, even while he did his homework. He would memorize poems and repeat material they've gone over in class, working out all the while, and he said that he remembered everything better this way. In the evenings, he would spend a long time striking his heels against a stack of newspapers he'd hung on the wall. He would jump, kick the newspapers with his heel, jump back and kick again. Every day he proudly tore off one newspaper from the stack with his teeth. One day, during yet another training session, when the newspaper stack on the wall had grown noticeably thinner, the paint started flaking off the wall, and the stack tore off the nail it was mounted on. He kept kicking his heels furiously against the bare brick. The adults came and painted the wall, but they didn't yell at him because they realized he hadn't done it on purpose. The laughed, advising him to train on the concrete wall of the garage. The armless boy would wake up before everyone else, go outside and hammer away at the blameless concrete wall. Now he could train his legs in the mornings too, without disturbing the others' sleep. He was a strong fellow.

Seryoga did have arms. He was developing his physique the usual way. Except that when he did the chin-ups on the bar, he wore a backpack. At first, the backpack held only a small weight to compensate for his missing legs' weight, but then Seryoga started adding dumbbells.

Even wearing a heavy backpack, though, he could do more than forty chin-ups in a set.

Even the physical education teacher liked the backpack idea. He started coming to workouts with one, too. Organizing children for the morning exercises was one of the physical education teacher's duties. Before, hardly anyone had gone to his class. That year, though, the PE instructor became the most influential teacher in the school. He was even more important than the math teacher. He helped the guys a lot and came up with fitness training ideas for the disabled. He warned us about overdoing and gave us long lectures on anatomy. He was a great teacher.

Serega was proud of his "pushers." "Pushers" was our name for the small boards with handles that the legless invalids used to push off as they wheeled around on their trolleys. Seryoga made his own pushers by himself at a labor lesson by welding aluminum pipes. These aluminum pushers with their rubber treads didn't stay light for long, though. Every evening Seryoga would light a small fire in the schoolyard, smelt some pig iron, and pour a little into his pushers. Every day, the pushers got heavier and heavier. He used them as usual. As always, he wheeled around the children's home on his trolley. Only now, he always carried convenient dumbbells at hand. By spring, each pusher weighed exactly five kilos. Seryoga decided to stop at five.

When summer vacation came, we gave Seryoga a very quiet sendoff. We could see that over the winter months of training, Seryoga had become very strong, but that meant absolutely nothing. Every time Seryoga achieved the next milestone, we understood that this was still not enough, nearly not enough. Seryoga worked out every day, but it was clear that somewhere out there, in his hometown, his enemy was working out, too, exercising every muscle of his intact body. When Seryoga managed to do fifty chin-ups for the first time, we were sure that his rival had done at least a hundred. If Seryoga pressed the dumbbell eight times with his left arm, his rival did it more like twenty times.

The summer passed quickly. Another children's home summer. In the autumn, as always, the parents brought their children back to the home. Seryoga has also returned. No one asked about the fight, and Seryoga didn't say anything. Not until one day, when Seryoga came to see the lads again, and Genka has introduced the subject casually. He said something vague about summer vacation. Seryoga understood right away, but got embarrassed and looked down. It was awkward to refuse Genka.

"There wasn't any fight," Seryoga said softly. "There wasn't. The first night I got home, I found him. He and some other guys were standing around smoking. I asked him if he remembered me, and he said he did. Then I swung my pushed at his knee with all my might. His leg broke and bent backward. He fell on the ground. He started screaming out, started calling for his mommy. I punched him in the gut a couple of times. He started gasping for air. I turned around to face his friend, but his friend already ran off to call the adults. What a rat! They came back with a doctor. They asked me what did I use to beat him up that much. I answered that I used only my hands. There was a big fuss. As it turned out, he had had a knife in his pocket."

"Then what?"

"Then was nothing. His father came over to our house. We sat down and had a drink. I told his father the whole story. And later, that guy and I got to know each other better. He is okay, only weak. He went around on crutches all summer. It's strange. I invited him to come fishing, and he said he wasn't allowed to go far on crutches. He's got strange parents, too. I tried to explain that half our children's home goes everywhere on crutches, but they didn't understand. And the fishing was good this summer. I caught a pike. Good fishing."

That evening the lads argued for a long time. They couldn't understand why that fellow with a broken leg hadn't fought. After all, he still two whole arms and a good leg left. And he even had a knife in his pocket. He was strange, and his friend was also strange.

The Bicycle

Lights-out. The adults turn off the lights and leave. The children are supposed to go to sleep. The best time of the day is a couple of hours after lights out. We are not sleepy. It's dark. If there is no holiday, there is no reason to turn on the light. A holiday is another matter. On holiday you can open cans of food you've stashed away, drink some wine, and if there isn't any wine, at least tea. If it isn't a holiday and you are not sleepy, you can talk. At night you can talk about anything you like, and no-one is going to laugh at you. At night you can think about home, your mama and papa. At night – you can. No one is going to say that you are weakling or a mama's boy. At night – they won't.

That night they were talking about their parents. I said nothing. Usually, when they ran out of things to talk about, they would ask me to tell them something interesting from a book I'd read. That night I didn't have anything to say. I listened.

As they did nearly every autumn, the boys were arguing over who has the best parents. Naturally, they all had fine parents—the best moms in the world, the strongest dads. Not everyone had a dad. Those who did had their very, very best.

"I have a great dad," one fellow began. "The very best."

"Weren't you telling us how he drinks?"

"So, what if he does? He is still great. This summer our neighbor gave his son a bicycle for his birthday. A grown-up bicycle, a two-wheeler. He let everyone take a ride. Everyone on our block took turns taking rides on the bicycle. My dad didn't drink for three days. He was thinking. He went around the house in a foul mood. Mom brought him a beer, but he wouldn't even drink beer. He picked up my notebook and pen and did some figuring. He went to the bookkeeper and then to the trade union committee. On Saturday, he went to the district center and came back sober. He brought me a radio. Here, he says, that neighbor our mine can only buy his son a bicycle for his birthday, but I can buy my family presents whenever I want. For two weeks he didn't drink. He asked to work the night shift, to make more money. It's a big radio, an expensive one. No one we know has anything like it. It has all the countries of the world written on the dial. You can pick up anything you want on it: music, children's programs. There is even a program where they read books for the blind. I listened to it every day—a fine radio. And my neighbor's bicycle broke pretty soon anyway. I've got a smart dad. He knows what to buy. Radio is better than a bicycle, after all. Right?"

No one even bothered to argue. It was obvious. A radio is a serious thing, whereas a bicycle... What's a bicycle? A hunk of steel with two wheels. That's all.

The Spanish Girl

The hospital. I am lying here in a cast up to my waist. I am lying on my back. I have been lying here for more than a year. I am looking at the ceiling. I have been looking at the same spot on the ceiling for more than a year. I have no desire to live. I am trying to eat and drink as little as possible. I am making an honest effort. I am trying because I know that the less often you eat, the less often you need to ask for help. Asking others for help is the most terrible and unpleasant thing in life.

Rounds. The doctor is going from ward to ward with an entourage of a very young student. He gets to my bed. He glances at my chart and recites what I have heard many times this year. He talks about my arms and legs and my mental retardation. I am used to it. They do rounds frequently. I have grown used to a lot in this hospital. I almost don't care. The doctor pulls back the sheet, takes out his pointer, and spends a long and tedious time showing the bored students my body, explaining to them the methods of treatment and other nonsense. The students are practically asleep.

"How much is two plus two?" he asks me suddenly.

"Four."

"And three plus three?"

"Six."

The students are cheering, almost waking up. The doctor explains to them briefly and convincingly that not all parts of my brain have been affected. "The boy even remembers his name and recognizes his doctors." He smiles at me. I know those kinds of smiles, and I hate them. It's the way people smile at very small children or animals. Insincerely.

"And how much is two times two?"

He puts special emphasis on the word times. This is too much. Even for me, this is too much. Even in this hospital, damn it.

"Two times two is four, three times three is nine, four times four is sixteen. I am cold. Pull the sheet over me or at least close the window.

Yes, I am retarded, I know that, but retarded people get cold too. I am not your guinea pig."

I'd heard the term guinea pig when they were redoing my cast. The doctor looks at me very strangely. He stands there in complete silence. A girl from his retinue quickly reaches towards me, pulls the sheet up, and walks away just as quickly.

Rounds are over.

That evening, a woman in regular clothes came to see me. She is young and beautiful. She is not wearing a lab coat. I haven't seen anyone without a lab coat for more than a year. She leans over me decisively and asks:

"Are you Spanish?"

"Yes."

"I am Spanish too. I am studying at the teachers' college. They asked us to retell The Tale of Igor's Campaign[1]. It is a difficult text, and I don't understand any of it. Can you help me?"

"But I am still little, and you are a college student."

"That doesn't matter."

"Okay, I will try to help you."

She takes a book out of her bag, pulls the chair over to my bed, and reads. She reads slowly, almost syllable by syllable. I know most of the "incomprehensible words," and there are handy notes in the book for the ones I don't. A fine book.

It's getting dark. She has to go. She closes the book and stands up.

"We still haven't gone through it all. I will come back tomorrow. My name is Lolita."

"I am Rubén."

She smiles.

"I know your name. I will come tomorrow, Rubén."

That night I can hardly sleep. No one has ever come to see me before. Nearly everyone has someone on the outside: parents, grandmothers and grandfathers, brothers and sisters. One Georgian fellow even had a visit from his cousin. His parents are dead, and his uncle is raising him. The Georgian explained to me that his cousin was his blood relative. And a blood relative, he told me, is the closest person on earth. He has lots of blood relatives. I don't have anyone.

---

[1] The Tale of Igor's Campaign is an anonymous epic poem written in the Old East Slavic language.

The next day the volunteers came to see us. The teachers' college had suddenly adopted the children's wing of our hospital for their volunteer project. That is, they'd probably had it formally before, but this time they came to our ward specifically. Among them, naturally, was Lolita. She had on a white lab coat over her dress.

She walked over to my bed.

"See? I came. Why are you crying?"

———— ◆ ————

The volunteers came often, almost every Sunday. Lolita wasn't always with them, but when she was, she would spend a long time sitting by my bed. We talked. We just had friendly chats. Talking with another human being meant a lot to me, too much for a child's psyche. An enchanting luxury. For her it was always not enough. Just coming to see a sick, lonely child was not enough. One time the students brought a movie projector to the hospital. They showed cartoons in the lounge; as always, I stayed in my room alone. Lolita came in, took a look at me, said something, and I said something back. She must be in a bad mood today, I thought. She quickly ran out of the room. The next Sunday students brought the projector into my room. She turned my bed sideways to face the wall. On a bright spot on the hospital wall, a funny wolf kept trying to catch a crafty rabbit: all ten episodes, ten episodes of the most famous Russian cartoon of all. I was seeing this cartoon for the first time in my life.

With Lolita everything was for the first time. For the first time, they moved me from the bed to the stretcher and took me outside. For the first time in my entire hospital life, I could see the sky—the sky instead of the eternal white ceiling.

———— ◆ ————

It was a holiday. A holiday in the hospital. The holidays didn't concern me. I didn't care about the holidays. Someone somewhere else was having a good time.

A very beautiful, brightly made-up Lolita ran into the ward wearing a Spanish costume and without her lab coat.

"Come on, Ruben, they are bringing the stretcher, and we are taking you to the lounge. Today I am going to dance."

She was beautiful and filled with joy. A walking, talking holiday.

A nurse came into the room—a regular nurse in a white coat.

"You can't move the patient. They operated on him recently."

Lolita's arrival made me forget about all my operations. Once again, the doctors have cut off my casts—more pointless pain. I couldn't. I could never do anything. Actually, I was used to it; I was almost used to the eternal can't. Lolita wasn't. She ran out of the room. She left.

A couple of minutes later, some people ran in noisily and started speaking Spanish – Lolita, one Pablo, and a short fellow with a mustache. Pablo had his guitar. I knew Pablo. The one with the mustache switched to Russian. "You are supposed to be at the event, immediately."

"I am going to dance here. Here and now."

"You are going to dance there, where they tell you. I am taking my guitar. Pablo, let's go."

"Are you going, Pablo?"

Lolita gave the tall fellow a provocative look. It was an openly challenging look, full of joy and defiance. Pablo looked down.

The fellow with the mustache left, leading unhappy Pablo away. We were alone in the hospital room.

Lolita was dancing. She danced, snapping out the rhythm with her fingers. Lolita danced. She danced for herself. Intensely and strictly, she tapped out a strange, exotic melody. Without a guitar and without Pablo. She danced for real, every part of her.

Dance troupes sometimes came to the children's home. The young fools would stomp earnestly on the stage of the children's home club. The master of ceremonies would come out on stage and announce another number, and the fools would stomp the stage differently. It was boring. Only once was the established order violated. Yet another dance troupe would come to visit us on Victory Day. For the umpteenth time, they cranked up the usual music. Suddenly our history teacher dashed out on stage and whispered something in the ear of the distraught accordionist. The teacher began to dance, squatting and kicking and jangling his medals. The girls stepped back for this war veteran and stayed out of his way. The man had been drinking, so let him dance. The teacher had indeed had a little to drink that day. That's what Victory Day was for. He danced well, with abandon. His performance seemed curiously intimate. He radiated freedom and strength. I never saw him like that again. But now I'd seen real live dancing for the first time, in a northern Russian hospital. Real dancing. Spanish dancing.

———— ◆ ————

We said good-by. Lolita had to leave.

"I will find you, little boy. I will definitely write you a letter, so wait for it." She promised to write, but I had no faith in her. Once again, I had no faith. "You won't be able to find me. I don't even know what home they are going to take me to."

I had no faith.

A couple of years later, a letter did arrive. A regular letter. The first letter I'd ever got in my life. In it was a beautiful card. On it was a Spanish girl dancing in a colorful dress. The dress on the card was decorated with colorful threads. They didn't make cards like that in Russia.

The teacher gave me a letter. She put an open envelope in front of me. She sat down, facing me.

"Ruben. You and I have to have a serious talk. I read the letter. There is nothing dangerous in it. Not yet. I hope you realize you can't write an answer. Spain is a capitalist country. Corresponding with capitalist countries is not recommended. Any foreigner can turn out to be a spy. You are a smart boy, and you have to understand that the children's home administration does not have a right to subject you to risk like that."

She took the envelope away and left.

I looked at the card for a long time. Then I hid it in my math textbook. The next morning my card was gone.

The Volga

The Volga. The great Russian river. There is a car called the Volga, too. There are many kinds of cars. When I was little, I thought there were only Volgas[1], Moskviches, and Zaporozhetses[2]. They wrote about other cars in books, but I'd never seen other cars.

Each year, in May, the children's home had a graduation party and invited graduates from previous years. Many of the former students came in cars. The teachers greeted them and were happy to see all of them, even those who came in "handicap" cars – cycle-cars with moped engines. They were especially happy to see the ones who came in Volgas. If a former student bought a Volga, he was special. At the ceremony, he was invited onto the stage and asked to deliver a commencement speech to the graduates.

Sometimes we talked about cars. The children argued over whose dad had the coolest car. Not all parents had cars, far from it. Some had motorcycles at home. Motorcycles didn't rate in our debates. Cars did, including the cars owned by grandfathers and older brothers. One boy didn't have a dad, but his mom had a car. He was very proud of his mother and her car. If someone's parents didn't live too far away and they came to the children's home in their own car, there was nothing to prove. It was harder for a boy whose family lived far away. He could show a photograph of a whole family in front of the car, of course. But who was going to believe the photo? If his dad mentioned his car in a letter, that was another matter. If his parents wrote that the car had a flat tire, that meant they had a car. Parents wouldn't lie. Why should they?

I didn't know at the time whether my dad had a car. I still don't. If we ever meet, I will ask. I didn't know at the time that I had the best grandfather in the world. The very best. That my grandfather was a general secretary of the Communist party. I didn't know that he fought

---

[1] One of the best cars in the Soviet Union. The car factory that produced it is located by the Volga river.

[2] One of the worst cars in the Soviet Union. However, most of the Soviet people could not afford it.

for the freedom of the Spanish people, that for a long time he'd lived underground. I didn't know he was friends with Picasso. I didn't know he was being driven around Russia in a black Volga.

If only he had come to see me just once. He would have arrived in our small town in his Volga. Everyone would have seen what kind of car my grandfather had. Maybe Picasso would have sent a picture – a small picture – through my grandfather. He probably wouldn't have wanted to give me a big one. But a little one? We would have hung that picture in our club, next to the other pictures, under the portraits of the Politburo[1] members. We already had pictures hanging there that the papa of one boy had drawn. The boy's dad was a designer in a factory. The boy was very proud of his papa and his pictures in the club. No, we would have had to hang the Picasso in the teacher's lounge or the director's office. Picasso was cooler than a state designer.

My grandfather would have come with the secretary of the district committee of the Communist Party of the Soviet Union. We would have assembled in the club. The director would have delivered a welcome speech and turned the floor over to him. Everyone would have found out that my grandfather was the very best Soviet agent in the world, like Richard Sorge or Stierlitz[2]. So what if Stierlitz was only in the movies? We were told that the real Stierlitz is alive and on a secret mission.

Everyone would have seen what kind of grandfather I had. The general secretary of the Communist Party is more important than a teacher, more important than a children's home director. He would have come out on stage and given a speech on the international situation, and everyone would have immediately realized that he was the most important person there, at home, in Spain. More important than you can imagine. You don't get more important than that, almost like Leonid Ilich Brezhnev.

He would have seen the top marks in my grade book and my photograph on the school's honor board. He would have loved me, his grandson, immediately. You see, he was a good man, my grandfather. The best grandpa in the world, like grandpa Lenin, like Leonid Ilich Brezhnev. We all knew that Leonid Ilich Brezhnev loved children very much and made sure every day that every Soviet schoolchild had a happy childhood.

---

[1] The Political Bureau—is the executive committee for communist parties. The ruling elite of the Soviet Union.
[2] Max Otto von Stierlitz was the spy character of the Soviet spy book and TV series titled "Seventeen Moments of Spring."

Maybe he didn't have time to come, though. Maybe American spies were following him. Maybe he was part of a conspiracy. He could have written me a letter or even sent a package. I would have received a package, a huge package of chorizo. I wouldn't have eaten the whole package myself. I would have given everyone a piece of Spanish sausage. The teachers and attendants too. I would give some even to our three-legged dog. Everyone would have eaten my sausage and been amazed. "What unusual sausage they have in Spain, don't you think?" they would have said to each other. Even the dog would have been amazed. But the dog wouldn't have said anything. Dogs don't talk.

Maybe he didn't have money for sausage. Maybe he, like grandfather Lenin, was hiding in a cabin. And maybe, like grandfather Lenin, he didn't eat anything, just drank carrot tea, and when workers and peasants gave him food, he didn't eat it himself, but gave away the last crumb to the children in the children's home. He could have called. He could have called the director of our children's home on a secret telephone. The director of our children's home was a communist, and communists always helped each other. They would have called me to the director's office and told me in strict secrecy about my grandfather, the very best grandfather in the world. I would have understood everything. I was a smart boy. All I needed to know is that he was somewhere and that he was on a secret mission and couldn't come. I would have believed he loved me and would come some day. I would have loved him even without the sausage.

Or maybe he was afraid of being found out. Perhaps he would have realized that American spies rarely look in on our small provincial town, and they would have allowed me to tell everyone about my secret grandfather. Tell them just a little bit. My life would have been entirely different from then on. They would have stopped calling me black-assed one, and the attendants wouldn't have shouted at me. When the teachers praised me for a good mark, it would have been clear to them that I wasn't just the best pupil in the school, but the very best, like my heroic grandfather. I would have been confident that after I finished school, they wouldn't take me away to die. My grandfather would come and collect me. Everything would have changed for me. I would have stopped being an orphan. If someone has relatives, he is not an orphan. He is a regular person, like everybody else.

———— ◆ ————

Ignacio didn't come.

———— ◆ ————

Ignacio didn't write.

———— ◆ ————

Ignacio didn't call.

———— ◆ ————

I don't understand him. I will never understand him.

Mental

The children's home. The right place. If you've ended up in a children's home, you are lucky. You'll graduate from high school and go home a different person, a completely changed person. You will have a diploma in your pocket and your whole life ahead of you. You have a whole life ahead of you. Not having arms or legs is small stuff. Look, your neighbor, Uncle Petya, came home from the war without legs, and he is okay; he is getting along. His wife is a beauty, and his daughter is educated; she is studying foreign languages in college. Uncle Petya did all right for himself: the war taught Uncle Petya life, and the children's home will teach you.

You will go home, drink 250 grams apiece with your father, and light up. Your father will understand everything. He served in the army, and he knows what's what in this life. Only your mom will cry. That's bad. When women cry, it's always bad. Don't cry, mama, everything will be fine for me, just like for other people. No worse than for Uncle Petya.

A children's home isn't just a housing. It's also a school, a good school. And the teachers are good. There are smart books and three meals a day. It's a good place, the children's home. Good friends. Real friends. Lifelong friends.

❖

They brought a new kid to the children's home. A walking one. JCP. Juvenile cerebral palsy. I have juvenile cerebral palsy, too, but everything was more or less okay with the new kid. Just an uneven gait, arms flung out to the sides. His face twitched in a continuous effort to hold back his drool. Smart or dumb – you couldn't tell from his face. The new kid was a puzzle. A new kid was always a puzzle, always a distraction.

The children's home had a funny tradition. When someone with JCP got distracted or lost in thought or was concentrating on something, you were supposed to creep up on him and shout in his ear. He would jerk sharply, and if he didn't keep his wits about him, he might fall off his chair. If he just jerked and dropped his pen, it wasn't that funny. It is best to wait until he was drinking hot tea or wine. Wine was the funniest of all. They could always pour him more tea, but not wine. It was his own fault. He's let his guard down.

I knew that weakness in myself – jerking from a sudden clap or a shout. Therefore, in an unfamiliar situation, I always tried to find an advantageous position to hide in a corner or crawl under the table. Precaution was a standard operating procedure. So what? It was a children's home.

The new kid walked into the room freely – too freely. He took off his backpack and collapsed on the nearest bed. His feet were facing the floor, and his hands were searching his pocket for a handkerchief, as usual. He got it out and wiped away the nonexistent drool.

Suddenly everyone barged in all at once and started laughing. His friends. His future friends.

"Are you the new kid? Why are you lying on my bunk?"

"J-just a sec. I'll get up. JCP."

He said "JCP" clearly, with meaning. You could tell he wasn't joking. He was having a hard time, and now he'd fallen on the bed.

"Well, get up, don't lie there. Classes are over. Now we are going to scarf down some food. Want some tea?"

They poured him a full cup of tea but took pity on him. So they plopped in a good amount of sugar. You could tell right away that they were good guys. That meant they'd accepted him. He summoned up his nerve, sat up, stood up carefully, and moved to a chair. He picked the metal mug up, even though it was still hot, and tried to take a sip.

"Paah!" a boy on crutches shouted very loudly – too loudly – in his ear.

He fell. His hand automatically flung the hot mug at his offender. It missed. If only it had hit him in the eye! It doesn't hurt to dream. Winning the lottery is rare. The mug cut the beast's temple. At most, he'd have a bruise, no more. A minute. Just a minute. Just a minute while they enjoyed a laugh together.

One, two, three...

Remember what you read about Cassius Clay or, as everyone calls him, Muhammad Ali? It doesn't matter. They still don't know. They can't imagine that there, in Chuvashia, you're the city boxing champ among the healthy. "Among the healthy" is a title you've awarded yourself. All the other titles, on the contrary, limit you. "World champ among the healthy" sounds like a personal insult. But you haven't insulted anyone. A referee couldn't find fault with that. If there's drool running from your helmet, it's from rage. If your arms are trembling and your legs are dancing – that's the trainer's tactics. Always stay in character. Support the image. Always play healthy. Undercut. In fact, you already know that healthy people aren't always healthy. That only sometimes do they make an effort to go after specific goals. But you're always making an effort. Now it doesn't matter whether you strike with the left or right, because your arms aren't working. But if you have to, if you really have to, you can make an effort, through the pain, the nervous tension, and the revulsion for the extra drooling. Then you can. Then you can do anything. You can do anything, and no one can stop you. Then – an accurate blow to your opponent's helmet. A good blow. Like always. Like your whole life. The usual. After all, no one applauds when you button your fly. They button their flies every day, and they don't get a medal for that. The mayor doesn't shake their hand at an official reception.

Four, five, six...

You have to get up. Your wet shirt and shoulder, now burned from the boiling water, is nothing. It could be much worse. Anything could happen. They could fall on you at night, cover you with a blanket and beat you. Just like that. Because you are the new kid, so you know your place. Or rush you en masse, out in the open. That's always better when it's out in the open. However, it is not evening yet. The night is coming, and they are going to beat you up. That's why you have to get up. Right now. Be strong and cruel. You don't want to fight, you don't want to fight at all, but you have to.

He got up. Oddly, they were still laughing. They didn't get it. He took a quick look around. He walked over to the boy who'd shouted in his ear. A little boy, a couple of years younger than him, frail, on crutches. Why did he do that? That is odd. He hit him; the boy fell down, the crutches flew up. He started beating him up. They didn't let him beat him for long. They jumped him from behind and pulled him off.

"What's the matter with you? He was joking. Can't you take a joke?"

"Y-y-yes."

Damn! The stuttering comes out in the worst possible moment. Now they think you are scared.

They let him go. He got up again. He slowly stood up and walked toward the boy lying on the floor. You have to beat him. Beat him for a long time. Then they'll believe you are serious. Then they will treat you like a human being.

"Where are you going? Cut it out. That's enough."

A boy stepped in front of him, apparently healthy, apparently his age. You can't always detect a disability right away, though. When he walked over, he seemed to be dragging his foot slightly.

"Cut it out. Cool it. My name is Hamid."

He took aim at Hamid. Okay, first the jaw – and he'd fall. Then he could fall on him and beat him for a long time. Not that they'd let him, of course. They'd intervene. Then he'd have to fight them all at once. Might as well get started.

Hamid understood immediately. He took a step back and smiled.

"What's wrong with you? Are you psycho? Now you are going to beat me? What did I ever do to you? Kolka was joking, just joking, and you hit him. You're even. That's enough."

"Fine. That's enough. Tonight I'll kill him. Or he will kill me."

Hamid smiled again.

"Have you been reading too many prison books? This is not a prison. It's a children's home. Just a children's home. No one kills anyone. And they don't fight much. Get it? Kolka was just joking. Why don't you sit down and drink your tea?"

"I've already had enough."

Hamid is wonderful. You can tell immediately he has a head on his shoulders and knows his way around a children's home.

"Want some wine?"

"I've got three rubles."

"You have money too?"

"Should I give you all of it right away?"

"Don't get angry; I was joking."

His lips started to tremble, and his head jerked a little to one side.

Hamid understood. He understood everything.

"No need. Don't get so worked up. Your money is your money. No one is going to take it away. They don't steal much either. What's your name?"

"Alexei."

"Lyokha, then?"

"Alexei."

Alexei took a step forward. He was going to have to fight after all.

"Fine. You are Alexei. But I can't call you Lyokha too? What's the difference? It's not an insult. Let's shake."

They shook hands.

"Bring anything to eat?"

Alexei smiled, took his heavy backpack from the bed, and tossed it on the table. He loosened the chords, and the backpack fell open. He laid out its' contents, and from the bottom of the backpack he took out two five-kilo dumbbells. He stepped away and sat down on the bed.

"Have at it!"

Hamid laid the provisions out on the table very deliberately. Salted pork, onions, garlic, a few cans of meat. No candies, nothing sweet. He pushed a jar of fruit to one side.

"My grandmother gave me the fruit. I didn't want to take it," Lyokha embarrassed and trying to vindicate himself, was almost stuttering.

"That's fine, you've got good food. And the fruit will come in handy, too. We will use them to sweeten the vodka. You didn't bring any cigarettes?"

"I don't smoke."

"Good for you. Neither do I."

◆

That night they drank wine.

They got out their knives and cut bread and salted pork.

Hamid made neat lard sandwiches and put one on the table in front of himself and one in front of Alexei.

Alexei was about to intervene, as if to say, I can use a knife myself, but Hamid didn't even begin to listen.

"Relax. There is no shame in getting some help. I can cut faster than you, right?"

Hamid got out the bottle and opened it. He poured himself a full glass and slowly drank it down. He poured a second for Lyokha.

"Can you handle a full one?"

"Put it in my mug."

He took an aluminum mug with an oversized handle out of his backpack.

"This new kid is not so dumb, he's got brains. The glass holds two hundred grams and the mug a whole four hundred."

"You don't get it. I can't lift a glass. Pour half a mug if you want."

"Whatever. I'll pour a full one, and you drink it. You'll skip a turn, that's all."

Alexei took his chair and moved it to the other end of the table, so he'd have his back to the window. He put a dumbbell on the table in front of him. Hamid poured a full mug of wine and put it on the table in front of Alexei.

It's not hard. Drinking from a mug isn't hard at all. You have to grab the handle with your right hand, press the left palm solidly against the mug, and drink slowly. It doesn't matter whether it's tea or wine.

No one said a thing while he was drinking. Not so bad, this new kid. The very first day, he drank down a mug of wine without taking a breath. Drank it all and put the mug down on the table. He took his handkerchief out of his pocket, wiped his face, and looked around.

Hamid offered Alexei a sandwich.

"A bite to eat?"

"Later."

"Don't take this wrong, Lyokha, but please get the dumbbell off the table. You are some kind of nut case, and you could still give someone a good wallop."

The wine had begun to take effect. Lyokha started laughing. He laughed loudly and merrily. He stowed the dumbbell under the table. He reached for his sandwich and began to eat.

It was a good children's home, a proper one. And the guys were good, too.

Father Frost

It's spring. I am sitting around with a friend—two high-school seniors in wheelchairs. My friend is smoking, smoking without bothering to hide the cigarette in his fist, or look over his shoulder when a teacher walks by. The teachers ignore him, too. Let him smoke. Let him do what he wants. He has myopathy anyway—a degenerative disease. No one knows how long he'll live. My friend is lucky. This spring they are going to take him home, for good.

"You know, Ruben. This year Father Frost[1] was fake."

"Are you out of your mind? What Father Frost? How old are you?"

"You don't get it."

He smokes his cigarette down and uses it to light his next. His slender, deft fingers carefully put the butt into a matchbox—slow, precise movements. I wouldn't be able to do that.

"You don't understand, Ruben. New Year's was when I first got really sick – that was before I started school. I still didn't know what was wrong with me. My parents called in Father Frost. He came late that night. I wasn't asleep, and they'd promised me Father Frost. Mama looked and saw that I wasn't sleeping, so she turned on the lights on the tree. Papa invited him into the kitchen, but instead, he came in straight to see me. He saw the medicine on my night table and the crutches. He said to Papa: 'What would we do in the kitchen? Let's sit and drink under your tree. My shift's over anyway.' They brought in the table, vodka and snacks from the kitchen. It was great. And they didn't make me recite poetry. They poured me a glass of lemonade. They each tossed back their first, and Father Frost took off his beard. A great Father Frost, we called him Uncle Petya. There just aren't any sober Father Frosts."

I knew what he meant. And I thought about my own Father Frosts. Old and young, male and female. The Father Frost, who was our lady literature teacher, and the young Father Frosts, who were students at

---

[1] Father Frost is a mystical figure that played the same role on the New Year's as Santa on Christmas.

the teachers' college. The Father Frosts, who were doctors – very often they were doctors.

Once in my life I saw a real Father Frost. He came in merry and drunk. Father Frost complete with a red nose. He said, "Hello, children," in a ringing bass voice. We answered the way we were supposed to: "Hello, Father Frost." Father Frost danced and sang. He recited poems. He looked at us boldly and attentively. He didn't avert his eyes from the tots in carnival costumes. When they turned on the slow music, he danced with an armless girl from the upper classes.

We reminisce. We reminisce about how the year before, a very young Father Frost read the children's names off a sheet of paper, got mixed up, turned red, and stammered, and the time came to pass out presents, all of a sudden, he didn't feel so good. They took him into the teachers' room and gave him valerian drops.

This other Father Frost was what we wanted. He left his magic wand at the door when he came in. He put the hokey sack of presents in front of the tots. The little boys didn't take anything out of the bag – they were too shy. Then he spilled all the candies on the floor right under the tree.

Toward the end of the holiday party, Father Frost went backstage. He returned without his beard and coat, wearing his dress uniform. He put on his glasses and took a piece of paper out of his pocket that has been folded in fourths. He read – he had a slight stutter – something about the Party and the government, about the ultimate victory of communism, about our happy childhood. Then, putting the correct paper back in his pocket, he made a loud announcement: "And now, my Snowmaidens will pass out presents to everyone!" He waited for the clapping to die down and walked off the stage and over to the small table where the children's home director was sitting. Young fellows with cadets' epaulets who didn't look anything like Snowmaidens carried big cardboard boxes of presents into the auditorium. They passed out all the presents very quickly and properly. To everyone – children and adults alike. It was a good New Year's, the best New Year's of my life.

My friend is smoking. I have been telling him about my own real Father Frost. We understand each other.

"You're right," he says. "There is no such thing as a sober Father Frost. Sober Father Frosts aren't the real thing."

The Dog

She came in all by herself. She turned in at the gate, struggled up on the bench, and lay there, wagging her tail. It was evening. Night, almost. An older boy who'd gone out into the yard for a smoke saw the dog. He was a grown man almost, a high-schooler. He put away the cigarette and quickly brought some water in a can.

Without words, invisibly, the news spread: "a dog." The usual routine flew out the window, and the children dashed outside, crowding around the bench. Each one wanted to pet and admire the dog.

Keeping dogs at the children's home was against health regulations. Dogs spread infections, and dogs can have worms. From time to time, some mutt would wander in and go over to the dining room. The children would sneak food to it, and the grown-ups would drive it away with sticks. That was all okay, all as it should be. In the morning, the dog would be gone. At night the truck would have come and taken the dog away. We were told they make soap from dogs. In the morning, the girls would come to school with tear-stained eyes. The boys didn't cry. Boys weren't supposed to cry. The high-schooler would smoke, though, hardly hiding it. They would smoke right in front of teachers, just asking for trouble. The adults tried not to react. The adults were sure that the children just needed time, that the children would forget everything. Smart adults.

Nearly everyone went outside. We stood or sat in silence.

An elderly nurse emerged from the clinic. She walked up and took a quick look at the dog.

"Take the dog away. The children need to wash their hands with soap and go to bed. Immediately. What's going on here?"

A boy on crutches, a preschooler. A Gypsy. He scrambled onto the bench and stood in front of the woman.

"You can't take her away. She is good. She came to see us all by herself."

The nurse looked at the child with disdain. She'd been around the block. She was used to this. She knew better. She knew exactly what these children needed.

"Go to bed, son. Who is on duty? Who is responsible for lights-out?"

There wasn't anyone on duty. The high-schooler who was on duty had gone to the toilet as a precaution and was sitting there, smoking and waiting.

The Gypsy stood there, confidently, hands on his crutches, his foot on the ground. He wasn't afraid of adults. He had the children's home behind him, the entire children's home. Right now, he had everyone behind him.

"You can't take her away! She is missing a foot."

The nurse knelt, facing the boy.

"Don't say 'foot,' say 'paw.' Understand? Dogs have paws, and people have feet."

She stopped short. She jerked her head back, stood up, and straightened her white coat. Her face was calm and intense. Not a trace of doubt. The face of a woman who was no longer young, but was certain she was right.

She went away and returned quickly. She opened her bag of instruments.

"Hold her."

The older boys held the dog down, and the nurse cut the dirty clumps of fur from her sides. She poured iodine on the open wounds. The dog shuddered, the boys held on to her, and the nurse did her job calmly and deftly. Toward the end, she used her sharp scissors to cut off a flap of skin on the dog's paw. She bandaged it up.

"Burn these clumps! Tomorrow we will call the veterinarian and give her all her shots. You have to change the dressing on her paw every day. I'll give you the bandages. If I see anything amiss – the dog will be gone. Do I make myself clear?"

She put away her instruments and went to the clinic. She gave a very young teacher aide a stern look.

"Everyone needs to wash their hands immediately and go to bed. Lights out."

If it was lights-out, it was lights-out. Everyone scattered. Only the Gypsy boy stayed with the dog. He was petting her on the head and didn't want to leave. The dog was wagging her tail sluggishly and looking placidly at the pieces of smoked sausage in front of her."

A teacher aide came into the yard and sat down beside them on the bench.

"Go to bed. It's late."

The boy didn't say a word.

She was a young teacher aide, just out of school. What kind of teacher could she ever be? She slid a little closer and reached out to stroke the boy's head, but he edged away, so she petted the dog.

"Go on, off to bed. Your dog has nowhere to go. I called the director, and he said he'd be watching your behavior and would decide what to do with the dog. They won't take the dog away. Not today, anyway."

The dog quietly ate her fill. Each of us wanted to feed the dog. The tots hid pieces of bread from breakfast in their pockets for her. The girls brought her the blini they made in cooking class. The sullen, hard-nosed boys from the high school brought her snacks leftover from their drinking parties. The cook – secretly at first, then openly – fed her kitchen scraps.

Over the winter, the dog grew a luxurious, rust-colored coat. That's what we called her – Rusty. The girls would brush her twenty times a day and braid her fur. She put up with all of it. She liked girls better than boys.

The boys played with her. The boys read books on animal training. The dog jumped through a hoop and stretched out her right, then left forepaw for a handshake. She knew commands "stay," "sit," "lie down." Her favorite command was "fetch." She could chase a ball for hours. She would put the ball right in the hands of those in wheelchairs. She played with everyone and went to everyone. If someone couldn't throw a ball, she would just rest her head on his lap. She was a smart dog. She understood everything and could do everything. She just couldn't walk on her one hind leg. Not that she had to do a dance for a piece of bread or beg to curry favor with people. They gave her food anyway.

One day on his way into work, the children's home director, a stern man with a big briefcase, leaned over the dog and ruffled her rusty fur. He asked her gravely: "How is life treating you? No complaints? Are your papers in order?"

Her veterinary papers were in perfect order. Everything about her was in order. She raced around on three legs and yelped cheerfully at strangers. She recognized us instantly, even those who weren't enrolled in the school yet and those who hadn't been in our home for very long. She distinguished us from strangers unerringly.

Sometimes stray dogs would pay us a visit. Now it wasn't just the adults who drove stray dogs away with sticks. Stray dogs were banned from the restricted territory of the home. Stray dogs had worms and fleas. We fired our sling-shots at stray dogs. In the spring, a man came. He said he was the former owner. We didn't believe him. He came in and reached out to pet Rusty. We believed him. That good dog hurled herself to the ground and started growling. Her menacing grown swelled into a howl. She pressed her belly to the ground and let up a howl. She jumped up, stuck her tail between her legs, and ran off to the furnace room.

On the first morning of her life in the home, the children had built a little house for her in the shop class. They had a special design for the doghouse: double walls and a warm wooden floor. The girls lined the house with old blankets. Someone brought a pillow—a pillow from home that didn't have the institution's stamp. The little boys carried cozy, homey things to the doghouse, their favorite toys. The older girls regularly handed all this back to the boys and chastised them, explaining that they shouldn't do that – it was pointless. From time to time, someone would bring cozy human presents to the doghouse anyway. She slept in that doghouse. She liked it. In the winter, when it was especially cold, the dog slept in the furnace room. Our very good-hearted stoker had once been a student in our home. He had arms and legs. He was a healthy, handsome man. Just not very bright. And almost mute. In ten years of schooling, he never did learn how to read or write. Who on earth needed him in that cold world of strangers outside our gate? When he was sad, he bought vodka. Vodka and ice cream. He drank vodka himself and shared ice cream with the dog. Often he sat there drunk next to the furnace, rambling on about something very important while the dog ate ice cream bar after ice cream bar. It felt good to be together. No one yelled at him for the vodka. Everybody knew that no matter how much he drank, the furnace would not go out. Even incredibly drunk, he conscientiously shoveled coal into the furnace—a fine stoker.

The stranger was waving his arms about, arguing, and making demands. The adults ignored his arguments. The adults threatened to call the police. He left and stood outside the gate, waiting for something.

The black-eyed boy with the shaven head, the sharp little Gypsy. He hopped along quickly on his crutches, wearing holes in the sole of his one boot. He came up, examined the stranger carefully, and tugged on his sleeve.

"Hey, buy my little knife."

He shook a penknife with a shiny composite handle out of his sleeve and into his hand. He threw his arm back – and the knife was gone. Lowered it – and the knife lay once again on his outstretched palm—simple gesture of the hand.

The man leaned towards the boy.

"Give it here. You are too young to be fooling around with a toy like that."

"Okay. Give me the money. It's my knife."

The boy threw the knife over his shoulder and showed him empty hands. He picked up his crutches and was all set to run away.

"Wait up. Call one of the older boys over."

A high-schooler came out. He was graduating that year. A tall boy with reddish bangs that fell right into his eyes and hair that covered his ears. His sleeve was neatly tucked into his belt.

They sat down on the bench by the gate. The boy took his cigarettes from his pocket, tapped a cigarette out of the pack, and grabbed it with his lips. Then he put a pack back in his pocket. He got out a matchbox. Steadying the box in his palm with his pinky, he deftly removed a match from the box with his thumb and index finger, struck it, and lit up. It all happened fast, very fast.

"So, what's on your mind?"

"Give me back my dog. I can see what's going on; I am not a little kid. She's had a good feed with you, and her fur has grown in. I'll give you a bottle of vodka."

"It's your dog?"

"Yes."

"Let's check that out. Was she born without her foot, or did she get that way? Watch me, I am going to figure this out."

"She got that way."

"So what, do you need her so badly for all of a sudden?"

"I am going to make a hat. You've fed her so well. She'll make a good hat."

"I see. All right then, bring the vodka and take the dog away."

"What do you mean, 'take the dog away?' You bring her out to me on the leash."

"Do you have the leash with you?"

"Of course."

The boy finished smoking and looked the man up and down. He was short, a head shorter than the boy.

"Hey, listen, why don't you buy my knife?"

"Is everyone here crazy? One of you already offered me his. Some snot-nosed kid."

"You are right, he is a snot-nosed kid, and his knife's crap. You should buy mine."

The boy lifted the hand with the knife to the man's face and pressed a button. The blade whipped out – a long, slender blade. With an almost imperceptible movement of his expert hand, he folded the knife back up and pushed the button again. He folded the knife up again and put it back in his pocket."

"Or maybe you need brass knuckles. Come to the gate after dark. Don't be shy. I make good brass knuckles. I won't charge you a lot."

"I need the dog."

"If you say so."

He stood up and went to the gate. He stopped for a minute, smiled, and suddenly beamed with joy. As if he had remembered something near and dear to his heart.

"Hey, listen, let's go right now, and you can take her away. For free."

The man cheered up.

"Let's go."

"Only you'd better watch out. She is in the furnace room right now, and the stoker's been drinking. He probably brought in a case of vodka yesterday. Our stoker is a pretty sturdy guy. He can lift a car by its bumper with one hand – doesn't need a jack. He is not quite right in the head, though. He doesn't hear so well. Just speak slowly, and he'll understand. And you know what? You should start with the main point, the hat. He'll understand about that hat."

The man finally figured out that they were fooling with him all along. He swore under his breath and slunk off. The children's home kids are one mean bunch, let me tell you.

————— ◆ —————

One of these days. One day I'll buy myself a dog. A smart Labrador, purebred, an expensive animal. He'll open doors for me and give me things I've dropped. Someday I'll forget this dog from the children's home. A fine dog, rust-colored, missing a paw.

Hands

I don't have hands. What I am forced to make do with can only be called hands at a stretch. I am used to it. I can type on the computer with my left index finger, and I can hold a spoon in my right hand and eat tolerably well.

You can live without your hands. I knew a guy without hands who has adapted pretty well to his situation. He did everything with his feet. He ate with his feet, combed his hair with his feet, and got dressed and undressed with his feet. He shaved with his feet. He even learned to sew on buttons. He could thread a needle himself too. Every day he trained his little-boy body. He worked out. In fights at the home, he could strike his opponent in the kisser or jaw with his foot without hardly trying— a normal children's home guy.

Living without hands isn't that hard if you have all the rest. All the rest – my body – developed even worse than my hands. My hands are the main thing. You might say that the main thing about a person is his head. Or you might not. Obviously, a head can't survive without hands. It doesn't matter whether the hands are yours or someone else's.

Sergey had hands. Two strong, perfectly healthy arms. Above his waist he was totally fine. Hands, shoulders, head. A blond head. Sergey Mikhailov. Seryozha.

In school he was one of the best students. That wasn't enough for him. He was constantly reading science fiction magazines, mailing entries in to contests for schoolchildren, completing assignments for magazines, and submitting them so that they would award him various certificates.

Below the waist his two twisted legs rested in a permanent lotus position. Below the waist he had no sensation, absolutely none, which meant he always had to wear a urinal. When the urine spilled from the bag, he changed his pants himself. He did everything himself. He didn't have to call for attendants, to demean himself, to ask for help. He himself could help others, the ones who were less fortunate. He fed one of his friends with a spoon, he helped him wash his hair and change his clothes.

He didn't have parents. He wasn't a walking one. When he finished school, they took him away to an old folks' home.

In the old folks' home, they put him in a ward with two old men. Harmless old men. One, a shoemaker, would heat shoemaker's glue on a hot plate; another, a goner, was completely out of it, and urine dripped from his bed. They wouldn't give Seryozha a change of sheets. They explained to him that he was supposed to change his pants once every ten days.

He lay in the ward for three weeks with the smell of shit and shoemaker's glue. For three weeks he refused to eat and tried to drink as little water as possible. Hooked up to his urinal, he couldn't crawl outside naked to see the sun for one last time. Three weeks later, he was dead.

In a year, they were supposed to take me to that old folks' home. Sergey had arms, and I didn't.

The Old folks' home

Since I was ten, I was afraid to end up a loony bin or an old folks' home.

It was easy not to end up in a loony bin. You just had to behave well, obey your elders, and not complain. Never complain. Those who complained about the bad food or objected to what the grown-ups did were periodically carted off to the loony bin. They would come back very quiet and obedient, but at night they would tell us terrible stories about the evil orderlies.

Everyone who couldn't walk ended up in the old folks' home. Not for any particular reason, just because. The only ones who escaped this fate were the ones who could acquire a profession. After graduation, the smart students went to colleges, and those who weren't so bright went to technical or vocational schools. Only the most hard-working and gifted students went to colleges. I was a better student than anyone. But I wasn't a walking one.

Sometimes after graduation, some non-walkers were taken home by their relatives. I didn't have any relatives.

———— ◆ ————

Everything changed for me after I learned that one fine day, they would take me to that awful place, put me on a bed, and leave me to die without food or care. The teachers and teacher aides lost their authority and wisdom in my eyes. Very often, as I listened to a teacher, I would find myself thinking that this might be the very person who would send me away to die.

They would tell me about theorems and equations, and I would automatically absorb the lesson's material.

They would tell me about great writers, but I was not interested.

They would tell me about Nazi concentration camps, and I would burst into tears.

When yet another attendant started yelling at me yet again, I would think with gratitude that she was right, she had a right to shout at me because she was taking care of me. There, where they were going to take me, no one would bring me a bedpan. She, this semiliterate woman, was good, and I was bad. Bad because I called for the attendants too often and because I ate too much. I was bad because I had been given birth to by a black-assed bitch who abandoned me to these fine, good people. I was bad. To become good took very little, just the tiniest thing— something almost everyone, even the stupidest person, could do. I just had to stand up and walk.

The teachers didn't understand why I cried all the time, why I didn't' want to talk to any of them, or write essays on the topic of my own choosing. Even the smartest and the best of them, the very, very best, refused to talk to me about my future. Other topics did not interest me.

———— ◆ ————

In the year when I finished middle school, they shut down the ninth- and the tenth-year grades. The high-schoolers were dispersed to other children's homes, and some were taken off to the loony bin. Children perfectly fine in the head were taken to a common loony bin. They were unlucky. As if often happens with people who have cerebral palsy, they had speech defects. The commission that came did not delve too deep and sent them off to a special institution for the mentally retarded.

I stayed on as the sole overage child. According to law, I had a right to ten years of schooling, but no one cared about the law.

They took me to the old folks' home.

———— ◆ ————

The children's home bus shook horribly as it rode over the bumps. The children's home director himself was taking me to the old folks' home. His broad smile revealed his gold teeth, and he was smoking Kosmos cigarettes, which were all he ever smoked. He was smoking and looking straight ahead through the window.

They lifted me out of the bus in my wheelchair. I was, after all, a privileged invalid. children's home graduates weren't supposed to keep their wheelchairs. They were taken away to old folks' homes without their wheelchairs, put in bed, and left to rot. According to the law, the nursing home was supposed to issue replacement wheelchairs within a year, but that was according to law. In the old folks' home where they took me, there was just one wheelchair. For everyone. Those who could crawl to it from their bed independently took turns taking rides in it. The rides were restricted to the building's porch.

It was autumn. September. Not yet cold. A low-slung wooden structure was built before the Revolution. No fence. Odd people wearing homespun coats and caps with earflaps were wondering around a yard overgrown with burdock.

A chorus was singing. An omnipresent chorus of elderly female voices. You couldn't see the old women; they were all inside. You could hear the singing coming from there:

Oh, the guilder blossoms
In the meadow by the brook,
A fellow young and handsome
I loved when first I looked..

Never. Never before or after, I have heard that kind of fatalistic plaintive singing. When I was riding on the bus, I'd been worried. After I heard the chorus, my worry subsided into apathy. I no longer cared.

They pushed my wheelchair inside. The hallway was dark and smelled of damp and mice. They steered me into a room, walked out, and left me there.

A small room. Bare walls. Two iron cots and a wooden table.

After a while, the children's home director walked into the room with an official from the old folks' home and an attendant. I could tell she was an attendant by her blue lab coat.

The attendant walked up to me. She examined me closely.

"But he is such a young, little fellow! What's going on? To think they are bringing us ones like this now! What's going on? People have completely lost their conscience!"

She walked out.

The director was smoking nervously and briskly, continuing his interrupted conversation.

"Won't you take him? It's really essential."

"Don't even ask. You must understand. He is sixteen now. Right?"

"Fifteen," I corrected him mechanically.

"Fifteen," the man conceded. "He is going to die here in a month, two at maximum. I only have the right to bury people who are at least eighteen. This is an old folks' home, understand? Where am I going to keep him for two years? All the refrigerators are broken. Broken, understand? And remember, do you remember what you told me a year ago when I asked for your help with the refrigerators? Do you? So don't ask. Take him to an asylum for the mentally disabled. They have the authority to bury infants if necessary."

"Don't decide right away; we'll talk. I need to make a call."

They went away.

I sat there alone. It was twilight. A cat ran down the hall.

Suddenly, the room was filled with a strange, disgusting smell. It stank more and more. I couldn't figure out what was happening.

The attendant was carrying a tray. She put the tray on the table and turned on the light. I had the honor of seeing the source of the strange smell. It was mashed peas. A green, sticky mass that looked as awful as it smelled. In addition to the peas there was a plate of borscht and a piece of bread on the tray. No spoon.

The attendant looked at the tray and noticed that the spoon was missing. She went out. She brought back a spoon. The spoon was covered with dried peas. The attendant broke off a crust of my bread, and carelessly wiped the spoon with it, then tossed the spoon into the borscht.

She walked over to me. She stared hard.

"No. He won't last the winter. That's for certain."

"Excuse me," I said. "Why is it so dark in here, and why is there a draft from the window?"

"This is an isolated room, a good room, and it's close to the stove. But they'll place you to the general ward for non-wakers. It's really drafty there. I told you, you won't last the winter. It's an old building."

"Do you have a lot of cats?"

"No, we don't have any cats."

"But I saw a cat run down the hall."

"That's not a cat. It's a rat."

"What do you mean, a rat? In the daytime?"

"What of it? Day and night. By day it's not so bad, but at night, when they run down the hallway, we lock ourselves in our rooms, and we are scared to go out. And they are nasty. A little while ago, they ate the ears of a bedridden old lady. Eat now, or it will get cold."

She walked out.

I brought the plate closer and ate the borscht mechanically. It was shit. The borscht was shit. The peas were shit. Life was shit.

I sat. I thought. Suddenly the director ran into the room.

He was rubbing his hands with glee.

"Well now, Gallego, we don't have to leave you here after all. Let's go back to the orphanage. Do you want to go back to the children's home?"

"Yes."

"Of course, you are."

He looked at the plate of food.

"You'll make it back by suppertime. And we won't be taking you to the psychiatric hospital either. Understand?" And he slowly repeated: "Ga-lle-go."

"Gonzalez Gallego," I corrected him.

"What's that? Like you understand a lot. I said Gallego, so it's Gallego."

We arrived at the children's home. We made it in time for supper.

"Come on, tell us, what is it like there?" a boy in a wheelchair asked me at supper.

"Tonight," I said. "I'll tell you tonight."

Language

A home. An old folks' home. My final asylum and refuge. The end. A dead end. I copy irregular English verbs into a notebook. They are carrying a corpse down the hall on a stretcher. The old men and women are discussing tomorrow's menu. I am copying irregular English verbs into a notebook. The other invalids my age have organized a Young Communists meeting. The director gave a welcoming speech in the auditorium dedicated to this latest anniversary of the Great October Socialist Revolution. I am copying irregular English verbs into a notebook. One old guy, a former prisoner, broke his crutch on his ward mate's head during his latest drinking spree. One old woman, an honored veteran of labor, hung herself in the closet. A woman in a wheelchair swallowed a handful of sleeping pills so that she could leave this regular world forever. I am copying irregular English verbs into a notebook.

It's all perfectly regular. I am not a human being. I haven't earned anything more than this. I didn't become a tractor driver or a scholar. They feed me out of pity. It's all perfectly regular. The way it should be. Regular, regular, regular.

Only the verbs are irregular. Resolutely and stubbornly, they etched themselves on the notebook pages after they made it through the rustle of static on the radio. I am listening to the irregular verbs of the irregular, English, language. They are being dictated by an irregular announcer from irregular America. An irregular person in a perfectly regular world, I am persevering in my study of the English language. I am studying it for no real reason, to keep from going crazy, to keep from becoming regular.

The Cane

The old folks' home. A terrible place. People shriveled by impotence and despair, their souls encased in an impervious shell. Nothing surprises anyone—the usual life of the usual poorhouse.

Four attendants were pushing a linen cart. An old man was sitting in the cart and wailing to break your heart. He was wrong. It was his own fault. The night before, he had broken his leg, and the head nurse ordered him to be moved to the third floor. For someone with a broken leg, the third floor was a death sentence.

His drinking buddies and other people he knew were on the second floor. On the second floor, they passed out meals regularly, and the attendants emptied the bedpans. The walking friends could ask a doctor or attendant to bring cookies from the store. On the second floor, you were guaranteed to survive if you had healthy arms. You could hold on until your leg is healed until you were a walking one again, and they kept you on the list of the living.

The old guy was shouting ominously about his service in WWII and explaining about his forty years' seniority in the mines. He was sternly threatening to complain to a higher authority. His trembling hands held out a handful of medals and decorations to the attendants. What a nut! Who cared about his trinkets?

The cart rolled slowly towards the elevator. The attendants weren't listening to him; they were doing their job. The old man's cry got softer, and his threats ceased. Clutching desperately to his useless life, he was pleading now, begging them not to move him to the third floor but to wait a couple of days: "My leg is going to heal up fast, and I will be able to walk." The former miner attempted to move the attendants to pity but in vain. Then he started to cry. For a moment, for just a moment, he remembered being a human being. In one convulsive movement, he grabbed the elevator door in a death grip. But what can senile hands do with the strength of four healthy women? And so, weeping and moaning, he was rolled into the elevator. That was it. A moment ago, there was a human being – and now there wasn't.

———— ◆ ————

Residents came to our institution by various routes. Some were brought by relatives; some came of their own accord, weary of struggling with the burdens of independent life. But it was the ex-cons who had the most confidence and the least ambivalence about being in a poorhouse. Ex-cons, tough old wolves, who acquired neither home nor family on the outside, would come straight to us after serving their prison term.

There had been a commotion and shouting since morning. The attendants have been swearing at a lively but withered old man, in vain. He hadn't intended to add to their workload.

It was the same old story. One minute, he has been playing cards and drinking vodka with his ward mate. Either his card hasn't followed suit or his neighbor had tried to cheat – who's to say – but the old man took his cane and whacked his drinking buddy on the head hard enough to splatter blood all over the room and then the toilet, where they had dragged the crippled card player and the hall from the ward to the bathroom. He hadn't meant to soil the floor, he hadn't, but that's what had happened.

As soon as the old guy had arrived at the old folks' home, he had filled his ordinary aluminum cane with pig iron and steadied himself with it when he walked. A thirty-year prison term had taught him to watch his back. And a good heavy cane isn't a bad thing to have in a fight. He liked his weapon, and he liked having at hand an absolute guarantee of his personal inviolability. But he was sincerely apologetic about the soiled floor. They forgave him, but to keep him from temptation; they moved him to a separate room.

———— ◆ ————

As usual, the attendants had raised a fuss a little earlier in the morning. Nothing too terrible. The ex-prisoner had had a stroke. A stroke was serious business. When the old man woke up, the right side of his body wouldn't obey his damaged brain. His right arm hung down like a rope, and his heavy right leg refused to move, a half-faced smile and a terrible sentence: the third floor. The fussy head nurse was running around giving orders. After they finished their breakfast, the attendants went off cheerfully, in no particular rush, to do their supervisor's bidding. There was no point in rushing; the old man wasn't going anywhere.

But the old ex-con was in no rush to reach the other world. He wasn't tired of the sun, and he hadn't drunk his full allotment of vodka.

Groaning heavily, he picked the cane up with his left hand and lay there, waiting.

The attendants arrived. They looked in amazement at the old man with his raised cane.

Before they could collect themselves, the old ex-convict took one look at them and started talking. He had the heavy, prickly gaze of a cornered beast. The heavy cane did not shake in his hand.

"What? Come to take me, bitches? Come on, get close. Are you going to be the first? Or you? I'll crack your head open, I promise. I may not kill you, but I will cripple you for sure."

He looked at them confidently, directly. The man understood that he was bluffing. What could he, a paralyzed man, do against four healthy country women? They could have fallen on him all at once and taken the stick away. Only no one wanted to be the first. They were afraid of injuries; they were afraid of his stick. After all, an ex-con would strike with no regret.

Without a moment's hesitation, the women exited. The head nurse ran up and down the hallway shouting at them, trying to coax them into it – in vain. They advised her to go in first and take away the old ex-con's stick.

In a helpless rage, the head nurse called the police.

The policeman on duty, a serious fellow a couple of years shy of his retirement, arrived at her urgent summons, military bearing, a pistol in his holster.

He walked into the ex-con's room and took a look at the disturber of the peace. On the bed lay a withered old man holding a cane in his hand for some reason.

"Are you disturbing the peace?"

"What do you mean, citizen officer, what peace can I possibly disturb? Don't you see how twisted I am?"

The policeman leaned over the sick man and threw back the sheet.

"Did they call the doctor?"

"The nurse came and gave me a shot."

"What do they need from me then?"

"You get the stick away from him, and we can take it from there," the head nurse broke into the conversation.

"Get out, citizen, and don't interfere. I am conducting an investigation," the policeman shut her up. He closed the door, moved the chair closer to the bed, and sat down.

"The guards in the slammer weren't as cruel as they are here," the ex-con tried to justify himself. "They want to move me to the third floor. That's where they have the goners' unit."

"What for?"

"Who knows? Women..."

"Women..." the policeman repeated thoughtfully. "I don't understand them."

For a while, they didn't say anything.

The policeman stood up and went out.

"All right, citizens. I have had an instructive chat with your patient. He promised to do better and not disturb the peace anymore. If he does something serious, have no doubt: we will come, write up the papers, and prosecute him to the full extent of the law."

He straightened his cap, gave the women in white coats a stern look, and walked towards the exit.

The old man recovered from the stroke after all. Whether it was the nurse's shots that helped or his ferocious thirst for life had pulled him back from the next world, he began sitting up little by little and finally got back on his feet. He would walk all over the place dragging his paralyzed leg, confidently holding his cane in his left hand. A good heavy cane. An excellent reliable thing.

Sinner

The old folks' home. The day flows into the night, and night flows seamlessly into day. Seasons run together, and time recedes. Nothing happens, and nothing surprises. The same faces, the same conversations. Only once in a while does familiar reality stir, rebel and spit out something completely unusual that doesn't mesh with simple, ordinary concepts.

She had lived at the old folks' home always, since the day it opened, it seemed. Modest and quiet, she was a little person in a big, cruel world. A little woman. No taller than a five-year-old child, her little arms and legs so loosely attached at her frail joints that she couldn't walk. Lying face down on a trolley, she pushed herself along, and that's how she got around.

The woman worked in the funeral services workshop. We had a shop like that in our house of sorrow. The old ladies made ornaments for the coffin, wreaths of artificial flowers, and other funeral tinsel for nearly all the deceased in a small town. Wreaths could be ordered at the workshop next to the cemetery as well, but it was generally believed that the wreaths there were more expensive and made any old way, without the proper respect for such sensitive and significant objects. Year after year, she twisted colored paper into neat little flowers, which she wove into cemetery wreaths, a respectful expression of touching concern for the dead.

No one ever insulted this poor woman. The employees never paid attention to her trolley as she went down the hall. She didn't ask for help and got to the toilet and cafeteria by herself. The rowdy drunks who, from time to time, terrorized all the poorhouse inhabitants would never have laid a finger on the defenseless creature.

And so she lived. She twisted flowers for the deceased during the day, and in the evening, she tatted napkins or embroidered linens, day after day, year after year. She lived just fine. She gradually adapted her small room to her own modest measurements, a mattress on the floor, a low table, a doll's chair, lace towels, and embroidered cushions.

She had lived a long time, too long. The woman was well past forty. She'd overstayed her welcome. At one of their meetings, the management decided that it was time to transfer her to the third floor. According to the usual schedule. The normal workings of a well-oiled machine. And on the third floor, they would put her on the ordinary big bed in a room with three goners and leave her to a slow death. They'd deprive her of her one luxury: the freedom to care of herself.

She'd lived her whole life quietly and had never asked the management for anything, but now, she suddenly signed up to see the director. She sat in lines for hours, and, having waited for her legitimate right to be heard, tearfully asked not to be evicted from her little room, begged to allow her to live out her days in familiar surroundings. They listened to her with a stone face, invariably refused, and later even began to banish her from the waiting line.

The night before the scheduled move, she hung herself on her door handle. Sinner.

The Officer

The brought a new guy to the old folks' home. A big man without legs, he sat on the low trolley. His gaze swept the area confidently as he rolled slowly into the building. He oriented himself immediately, without any help. He rolled around our entire three-story building, taking his time, section by section. He started with the cafeteria. It was dinnertime. He looked to see what they were serving, gave a grim chuckle, but didn't eat. He took the elevator to the third floor – the mortality floor, the goners' section. Without panic or fuss, he looked into each room and didn't hold his nose or turn away from the truth. He saw the helpless old men lying motionless on their beds and heart their moans and cries. Before nightfall, he returned to the room he'd been assigned to and lay down on the bed.

It was a nice room on the second floor, with one roommate. On the door, there was a handsome plaque with the inscription: HERE LIVES A VETERAN OF THE GREAT PATRIOTIC WAR. Decent living conditions. You could go to the cafeteria three times a day, eat what they are serving, and in the evening watch television with everyone. An appropriate portion of his pension would pay, with interest, for an elderly man's obvious needs – cigarettes, tea, and cookies. No one and nothing would keep him from buying vodka if he wanted to, or from drinking it with a neighbor reminiscing about the past, as they told each other what kind of men they'd been, how they fought in the war and won. They always won. As long as he had strength in his hands, he could push his trolley to the toilet and hold a spoon, and as long as he had lived, he could fight daily for the right to consider himself a human being.

That evening they didn't have any vodka. His roommate was good-hearted. All evening and half the night, this quiet old man, who had made peace with this barracks life, listened to the new man's story. In the clear, commanding voice, the legless man described his entire life in detail. No matter how his story began, though, it always boiled down to one thing: he has been a deep-reconnaissance intelligence officer in the war.

Deep-reconnaissance intelligence officers. Brave tested fighters, the best of the best, tops. The elite. They picked their way through the minefields into enemy territory and went deep into the rear. Not all returned, but those who did went into the enemy's rear over and over. War is war. They never ran away from death; they accepted their missions; they did what they were told. Death wasn't the worst thing that could happen to a man. They feared captivity – the disgrace, the humiliation, the helplessness. There were no prisoners or wounded in deep reconnaissance. According to regulations, anyone who was slowing the group's advance was supposed to shoot himself—a correct instruction. The death of one is better than the death of all. The wounded one killed himself, and the others went on – to complete their assignment and strike at the enemy. To take revenge for their country, for their dead friends, for the fact they had voluntarily taken leave of this life for the sake of the common cause. If an injury was severe that the soldier couldn't shoot himself, there was always a friend by his side who was compelled to help. A real friend, not a blowhard, not some drinking buddy or someone who happened to live in your apartment building. Someone who wouldn't betray you, who would share his last crust of bread and next-to-last bullet.

The officer went on and on with his story. About how he'd stepped on a mine. How he'd pleaded with his friend: "Shoot me." The accident had happened close to the border, so his friend carried him back to their territory, ten kilometers or so – not the deep rear. How his whole life he'd feared being a burden, how he'd worked in a cooperative, sewing stuffed animals. He'd married and raised children. He had good children; only they didn't need a legless old man.

And before the dawn, the officer cut his throat with a penknife. It took him a long time. He had a small dull knife. And his poor roommate heard nothing even though he was an old man and slept lightly, not a sound, not a moan.

The deep reconnaissance intelligence officer died. He died properly, by the book. Only he hadn't had a friend, a real friend nearby to smoke one last cigarette with him, to hand him a pistol and step aside tactfully so as not to interfere. No, he hadn't had a friend by his side. What a pity.

The Feeder

The old women liked to die in the spring. People died in all seasons, in a steady trickle, but most of all, they died in the spring. In the spring, it got warmer in the wards. In the spring, they opened door and windows, letting fresh air into the old folks' home's frowzy world. Life got better in the spring. All winter, the old women clung stubbornly to life, waiting for spring so they could let go and surrender to the will of nature and die in peace. There were far fewer old men in the old folks' home. The old men died without regard for the seasonal changes. If life refused to tempt them with a bottle of vodka or a tasty snack, they went to the next world without a fight.

———— ◆ ————

I am sitting in the backyard of the old folks' home. I am sitting alone. I am not bored. I am not bored at all. I am looking at spring. I am young, and I am certain I will live many years more in this world. For me, spring doesn't mean what it does for the old folks.

Someone appears in the doorway. A decrepit old woman is walking, pushing a chair in front of her. Violently she jerks her entire body straight and balances for a moment on her leg while her hands move the chair a few centimeters forward. Then, leaning heavily on the back of the chair, she slowly drags her feet toward it. After taking a look around and failing to spot any familiar in the yard, she moves confidently in my direction: one more companion, one more story.

The old woman comes up to me, stops her chair in front of my wheelchair, and sits down slowly and heavily.

All through the war, she worked on a collective farm[1] and worked from the morning till night. They weren't paid money. What money? They had one objective: everything for the front; everything for victory. On workdays they were issued groats. They made hot cereal out of the

---

[1] An ugly result of the Russian socialist revolution. All farmers in the Soviet Union mandated to work on collective farms (kolkhozy) or government farms (sovkhozy).

groats. Cereal, nothing more. Not even bread. After the war, things got a little easier because her husband came home alive and unharmed. She and her husband applied to move to the city. Her husband became a driver, and she went to work in a sewing factory. In the city, her husband quickly drank himself to death. The woman recalled her years in the city as the best of her life. She worked eight hours a day, and then she was free.

There was a meal every day at the factory: a first course, a second course, and compot. Life was good. After work, the whole collective would go and stoke the furnaces at the construction site, voluntarily. They called this the Young Communist Conscription. With pride, she listed the new construction in the city where she had made her contribution. They would stoke the furnace late into the night, and in the winter, they would work under the light of searchlights. All because they wanted to and enjoyed it. In the evening, she'd come home, eat something, and fall into bed. In the morning, it was back to the factory—movies on Sundays. Life has been good.

She'd retired at sixty. Her vision had grown weak, too weak for the sewing factory. Half a year later she'd had a stroke. Her neighbors took her to the old folks' home. She thought this is it, the end. Then her ward mate asked her for something to drink. Slowly she got up and helped her neighbor – and drank a little herself, and that seemed to make things easier. She looked around her, in the old folks' home. Everything was fine; she had a roof over her head and food. The only drawback was that it was all fine only as long as her legs held out. If you took to your bed here, no one was going to come to you. They put a plate of hot cereal on your night table – and then you are on your own. Even if you shouted, no one would come. She was scared. Her hands were accustomed to work; they wanted something to do. She started going from room to room, spoon-feeding the bedridden. After breakfast, she would start her daily rounds. Before she could feed everyone breakfast, it was time for dinner, and after that, supper, day after day, from breakfast to supper. She never did manage to feed everyone. She has made the decision to feed only the weakest, those who are dying. For those who were a little stronger, she would bring bread from dinner and put it into their hands. Bread in hand–you would not die.

It stank in those rooms: the smell of decay and death. The old women often asked for the bedpan, and some her to change their sheets. They asked for bedpans more often than food, more often than water. But she wouldn't. She'd decided once and for all that she was only going to feed them.

She would peek into the room and asked whether anyone needed feeding. People reacted differently to this innocent question. Some responded proudly, with metal in their voices that everyone in their room was ambulant; they even screamed and cursed at the feeder. It was an evil omen: The feeder is here – death can't be far behind. It didn't bother her. She just kept going from room to room.

The worst of all were those who really needed help. Those who, when they had strength, have yelled at the feeder, cursed her, and drove her away. Now, when they become helpless, they called for help more loudly than anyone else, begging her to feed them, and getting angry when she was late for dinner. They gulped down their food, spoon after spoon, keeping an eye on their portion, making sure the feeder didn't snitch any for herself. They lay there like that for a long time, in urine and feces. They rotted away until they had bedsores and ulcers. But they lived. They lived for years. They lived, losing their minds, not recognizing their benefactor, but persistently opened their mouths to meet the spoonful of cereal, swallowing greedily, staring into space with their uncomprehending gaze.

It was twilight. We didn't even notice half the day passed.

"How many years have you been feeding people, Granny?"

"Thirty-two. Easter, it will be thirty-three. I've got it all counted up. All of it."

"You are a hero," I said with admiration. "Thirty-two years! Serving people selflessly!"

"Selflessly?"

The feeder shook with delicate, soundless laughter. She quickly crossed herself three times and whispered a prayer.

"You, young people, are really stupid. You don't understand a thing about life or death."

She looked at me sternly with nasty little eyes. She examined my hands carefully.

"You eat by yourself?"

"Yes."

She sighed. I could tell she was dying to share her secrets with someone.

Without looking me in the eye, she spat it all out in one breath, precisely and sparingly."

"Selflessly, you say? There were cases when they'd offered me money. Not everyone lying here is an orphan. Their relatives would come and push their filthy money into my hands. Only I wouldn't take it. If they slipped it into my pocket, I would give it back to the old folks, down to the last kopek. I bought candies for the ones who couldn't think anymore and fed them every last one. I don't need their money on me, and I don't need their gratitude. I made a pledge. When I first came here, I fed out of foolishness, for no real reason. But one day, I came to feed one woman and she said to me: Give me the bedpan. I said – I don't give bedpans, I just feed. Fine, she says, feed me. She filled her mouth with bread, chewed it up, and spit it into my face, all over my face. And now, she said, tie my scarf tighter under my chin, so my mouth doesn't fall open when I die. I came to her every day, thinking she might change her mind, but she would just give me a stern look and turn away. She lay there for two weeks, dying. That was when I made my pledge that I would feed everyone if I could. Lots after her refused to eat, and I got used to it. It's just that first one I remember. And I made a pledge to die quietly, not to suffer. I am weak; I won't have the strength to spit out my bread. But lying there in your own wet is terrible. It gave me a bad scare. And you say 'selflessly.'"

The Pass

The old folks' home. Not a dormitory or a hospital. A sturdy wall of reinforced concrete slabs and a steel gate; located in the out-of-the-way part of town. Our neighbors are the lawbreakers in the minimum-security correctional facility next door. It's all out in the open there: prisoners and barbed wire. The prisoners have it good. They serve their sentence and go free. We have nothing to hope for. It's a closed institution. Entry is prohibited to outsiders. The residents don't have the right to leave the institution's gate without written permission from the director—formal written permission, with signature and stamp. The entrance gate is carefully guarded by a former guard from the neighboring prison. He is too old to work for the prisons, but he is still good enough for our gate. Sit there and open the gate for the bosses—a simple job, familiar, and not a bad bonus to his pension.

If you are healthy and agile enough, you climb the fence or dig your way out. For us, the invalids in wheelchairs, this wretched guard was a real Cerberus.

One young disabled man called a taxi. He got his friends to agree in advance to put him in the car. Three days before his trip, he'd obtained a pass. Everything was in order; everything had been planned out: they'd put him the car here, and he'd be met there. He was already in the car, and his folding wheelchair was in the trunk.

They drive up to the gate. The driver honks. The short old man with sharp nasty eyes takes his time coming out of his guard booth.

"Who is in the car?"

The driver doesn't understand the question.

"A person."

"Does he have a pass?"

The nervous driver takes the piece of paper from the invalid and hands it to the watchman. The watchman studies the document closely with a practiced eye.

"All in order, let him pass. I recognize him; he hangs around the gate a lot. Only the last time he was in his wheelchair and didn't have a pass."

"But he does now, right? Open the gate."

"You didn't hear me. It's written here, 'pass to leave the territory of the nursing home.' That's the document. I have to follow it precisely. If he wants to walk out, let him; if he doesn't, he doesn't have to. He can't leave the territory in a car."

The driver is irritated. He is not young anymore, and he is not accustomed to losing. He reverses the car toward the building and goes inside. After wrangling with the director for half an hour, he comes out holding the same pass, but with an addition in ink in the margins: "and to ride out." In the corner, the institution's seal has been added. The invalid is happy. The director must have been in a good mood that day. According to regulations, the pass should have been canceled, and a new application for a pass submitted, and he would have to wait several days for a decision on this tough question. The car drives up to the gate a second time. The watchman closely examines the amended document, returns it to the taxi driver, and goes reluctantly to open the gate.

They ride in silence for a few minutes. Suddenly the driver stops the car. He grips the steering wheel with both hands and takes a deep breath. Tensely, without looking at his passenger, he speaks almost angrily into the air in front of him.

"Here is the deal, buddy. Please don't take this wrong, but I don't want your money. And it's not because you are disabled. When I was young, I did three years, and I'll remember it my whole life. I've hated the fuzz ever since."

He flips off his meter and steps on the gas. The car barrels along at top speed, away from the old folks' home, the prison farm, and that bastard of a watchman. This is great. Freedom.

The Fool

A bus stop. My wife and I are going somewhere. We are waiting for the bus. The bus finally comes and at the wheel is a young fellow wearing stylish sunglasses. Alla picks me up, puts her right foot on the step, and shifts her weight onto it. All of a sudden, the driver smiles in our direction and steps on the gas. The sharp jerk spins Alla around, but she jumps on to the ground with me in her arms. She lands on her feet; her judo training serves her well. Then she straightens and puts me back in the wheelchair. A drunken fellow at the bus stop can't contain his laughter. He laughs long and gaily, and then he approaches us. Alla walks away. She doesn't understand how I can talk to such people.

"He is a fool," he tells me, "a fool, that bus driver."

"Why?"

"Because you have this wheelchair here, and you can see the sun and the birdies on the sidewalk, and what shape he will be in after some accident, nobody knows. He has a dangerous profession."

I get it. I smile. That driver, he really was a fool.

Playdough

It's easy to make a papa. Easier than making a mushroom. All you do is roll out two round pieces of playdough.

———— ◆ ————

When I was little, we made things out of playdough. The fat teacher aide gave us each to pieces. One piece we were supposed to roll into a snake, the other into a thin pancake. If you put the snake and the pancake together, you got a mushroom—a simple assignment for kids who are not babies anymore.

I put my hand on the playdough. I pick up one piece with the other. I try to roll the playdough out on the table. No success. I roll the piece over the table but does not get any thinner or thicker. I pick up the other one, with the same result.

The other children are coping with their assignments with varying results. Some mushrooms are coming out straight and handsome; others, small and crooked. The teacher aide goes around, giving each one of us advice, fixing the caps on some mushrooms, and the stems on others. The teacher aide comes over to me.

"What have you come up with?" she asks me gently.

I place one piece on the other. I feel my contraption now bears at least some resemblance to a mushroom.

"And what is this? What have you made here?"

The teacher aide takes my playdough and molds it with a quick, deft movement of her healthy fingers.

"Now, do you see what needs to be done?"

I nod. Now I see.

"And now, children, let's see who has the prettiest mushroom. Ruben has the prettiest mushroom."

I stare at the table. The mushroom in front of me is indeed the straightest and the most realistic. I don't care. It isn't my mushroom.

———— ◆ ————

My daughter is making a papa. It's easy to make a papa. Easier than making a mushroom. All you need to do is roll out two round pieces of playdough: two identical pieces, the two wheels of a wheelchair.

———— ◆ ————

"And now, children, let's see who has the prettiest mushroom."

Never

Never. A horrifying world. The scariest word in the human vocabulary. Never. The only word comparable to it is death. Death is one big never. The eternal never, death sweeps away all hopes and possibilities. No maybes or what-ifs. Never.

I'll never climb Mount Everest. I'll never go through long training periods or the necessary medical testing, travel, and hotels. I won't curse the weather, the slippery paths, or the steep ledges. There won't be any intermediate stages, mountains big and small – there won't be anything. Maybe, if I am lucky, if I am very lucky, I'll see Tibet one day. If I am incredibly fortunate, they will drop me off from a helicopter to the first staging point, at my first and last impossible. I'll see the mountains, the crazy climbers challenging themselves and nature. After their return – if they are lucky and they do return from the mountains without loss of life – they'll tell me joyously and a little abashedly how it all was, there, beyond the bounds of my never. They'll treat me kindly, I know. I am just as crazy as they are. It will be great. Only I'll never climb to the top myself.

I will never descend in a bathysphere to the Mariana Trench. I won't see how beautiful it is there, at the bottom of the sea. All I can have is videos, documentary confirmation of someone's else persistence, and heroism.

They won't take me into outer space either. I am not wild about barfing from dizziness or floating in a cramped metal box. It is not that I want to, but it hurts not to able to. Someone is flying there, over my head, and I can't.

I'll never sail across the English Channel. It won't work to cross the Atlantic in a raft, either. The camels of Sahara and the penguins of Antarctica will have to make do without my attention.

I won't be able to go to the sea in a fishing trawler; I won't see a swimming whale, calm and confident in his superiority. They bring me fish straight to my house, bring it in the best possible shape, filleted and ready to cook. Canned food, endless canned food.

I touch the joystick of my electric wheelchair and pull up to the table. I take plastic straw in my lips and lower it into the glass. Oh well, if it's prepackaged, then it's prepackaged. Slowly I drink the red wine – prepackaged sun from far-off Argentina. I turn on the television with a click of the remote. I mute it. One channel has a live broadcast of a young people's concert. The little people on the television are happy; they are singing and dancing.

The camera pulls back for a long shot. That guy with the tattoos and earring, I am sure, is trying to run away from his never, too. Not that it makes me feel any better.

Bro

Some friends and I – we are trying to get out to the country. There are no buses, and the heat is terrible. There is no point in trying to catch a ride. Three healthy guys plus an invalid in a wheelchair – who would pick us up?

Unexpected luck – an army bus. We have to choose; we have to try to get in. The guys lift me and the wheelchair up and try arguing with the driver. The driver keeps saying something about "I am not supposed to" and "regulations."

A soldier hurls himself toward the driver from the bus's depths, shouting, "Bro-o-o!" He is desperately drunk and angry. They argue briefly, and we are on our way.

The new recruits give us a seat. I am half-reclining on a low bench, which hurts. My "bro" comes up. He can barely stand; his tunic is unbuttoned, and under it is a striped sailor's jersey.

"Are you from Afghanistan?"

"No."

"Doesn't matter. Before Afghanistan, I didn't know what invalids were. Then my friends started coming home without arms and legs, blind. Lots of them couldn't take it and give up. How are you doing?"

"I am really doing all right. I've got a wife and a job."

"Hang in there. Live."

We get to town. They lift me out. He shouts something through the glass.

I'll remember you, bro.

I'll remember everything. I'll remember your jersey and your wild eyes.

I'll remember you, bro.

I'll hang in there.

Big Mac

In a fluent, energetic voice, the TV star with a Hollywood smile talks from the screen about the advantages of American democracy. I am not listening. I know what she is going to say. I am convinced she is right. She can be proud of her homeland. Its Constitution, anthem, and flag. She has the Bill of Rights, the Statue of Liberty, and McDonald's.

She gives the upbeat spiel about the famous fast-food chain. A sad-eyed clown with an idiotic grin looks at me from the colorful poster. A sandwich and a soda – what could be simpler? A slim American woman in a business suit tries in vain to convince me that this sandwich is the best sandwich, that this soda is the best soda in the world. Nonsense! Food quality is not the most important thing in my life.

I know that all McDonald's restaurants meet international standards for barrier-free access. I know that my wheelchair will move easily through all their doors. The most gracious employees in the world will help me use the toilet, cut my famous Big Mac into small pieces, put a handy straw in a cup with a lid, and lift it to my mouth.

That's it. That's enough—more than enough. For a paralyzed person, it's too fabulous a present. A sandwich and a soda. Bread and water. The very basics. Each citizen's guaranteed right to a place under the sun.

Democracy.

"I Go"

The English language. The language of international communication and business negotiations. You can translate almost anything into Russian. From Shakespeare's poetry to a refrigerator manual. Almost anything. Almost.

———— ◆ ————

A wheelchair. An American wheelchair. I have a joystick in my hand. The obedient machine moves my motionless body down the street of a small American town.

I cross the street to the red light. That is not surprising. I am crossing the street for the first time in my life. The wheelchair still isn't entirely obedient to the commands of my paralyzed hand.

The cars wait.

A delighted driver sticks his head out of the car, which is the far left-hand lane. He waves and shouts out words of encouragement.

A policeman walks up. He's guessed from my crazed look why I've broken the rules.

"Everything okay?"

"Yes."

"You are absolutely right to go outside! Good luck to you!"

———— ◆ ————

A woman in a wheelchair raced past me at full speed. She has a breathing tube in her mouth. Her wheelchair's back has been lowered to a horizontal position so she can watch the road through a mirror attached to the wheelchair. One the side of the wheelchair is a colorful message in big letters: I LOVE LIFE.

———— ◆ ————

A small Chinese restaurant. Narrow doors, four little tables.

The waiter runs out.

"I am so sorry. Please accept our official apologies. Unfortunately, your wheelchair won't go through these doors. If it's not too much trouble, you can go into the next room. You won't lose out at all, I assure you. It's the same menu, the same décor, the same chef. We have our certificate; you are welcome to read it. No discrimination here."

I make an embarrassing attempt to calm him down and assure him that it's no trouble at all for me to go to the next room. He accompanies me to the entrance.

This room is a little bigger. The waiter escorts me to a free table, moving the chairs out of my way.

A few restaurant customers clear their feet from the aisle, but some pay no attention to my chair. When the wheels go over someone's feet, he yelps. No surprise, given the wheelchair's considerable weight. We exchange apologies.

The waiter looks at me in confusion.

"Why do you keep apologizing? You have the same right to eat at this restaurant as they do."

———— ◆ ————

A young American girl in a wheelchair proudly shows me her van with a lift and tells me that all taxi fleets in America have vans like this.

"Couldn't they have reequipped ordinary pickup trucks for the disabled? That would have been much cheaper," I say.

The girls look at me in distress and embarrassment.

"But in a refitted truck, you can only take one person in a wheelchair. What if it's a boyfriend and a girlfriend? You mean you think they should ride in different cars?"

You can translate almost anything into Russian. From Shakespeare's poetry to a refrigerator manual. Almost anything.

I could go on and on about America. I could go on and on about the wheelchairs, the talking elevators, the smooth roads, the ramps, the vans with lifts. About the blind programmers and the paralyzed scientists. About how I cried when they told me I had to go back to Russia and leave the wheelchair behind.

But the feeling I experienced when I put the miracle of American technology in motion for the first time can best be conveyed by the brief yet condensed English sentence "I go." And that's something that doesn't translate into Russian.

But the feeling that I experienced when I first put myself in motion using the miracle of American technology can be best conveyed by the brief and capacious English phrase: "I go." And that's something that doesn't translate into Russian.

Homeland

Katya and I shop in a small shop for food. Katya goes to the back of the store while I wait by the entrance. All of the traveler's checks are made out to Katya since it's hard for me to sign my name. I have a hard time grasping a pen, and my signature doesn't inspire confidence anyway. Katya chooses the food and goes up to the cash register to pay. An elderly Arab is standing behind the counter. He starts arguing heatedly about something with Katya, gesturing wildly. Katya doesn't speak English, and it's up to me to sort this out.

I touch the joystick of my wheelchair and roll up to the counter. Katya steps aside.

"What's the matter?"

"I can't take your check. I don't take checks over ten dollars, and you are giving me one for fifty."

I am in America. I have been in America for two weeks. I am calm. I touch the joystick of my wheelchair again. The back of my chair comes up to almost a vertical. I ride right up to the counter.

"I see. You mean the check is forged. Look at me. Do you think I am capable of forging a check? Do I look like an artist? Do I look like a crook? Look at my wheelchair. Do you know how much a wheelchair like that costs? I bought food from you yesterday; I bought food from you the day before. I am buying it today, and I hope I will buy it tomorrow. This is America. You sell, and I buy. It's one or the other. If the check is genuine, you sell me your goods. If the check is forged and by me, then call the police."

He looks at me respectfully. This approach to business clearly suits him.

"Fine. I will take your check. Are you a Palestinian?"

"No. Spaniard."

"From Spain?"

"From Russia."

"When are you going home?"

"In three days."

"You must miss your homeland and be looking forward to going home."

"No, I don't miss it."

"Why not?"

"It's bad there. There aren't any wheelchairs, or sidewalks, or stores like yours. I don't miss it at all. I would stay here forever if I could."

He shakes his head reproachfully and looks at me with disdain and a little sadness.

"A boy, you are just a boy. What do you know of life? You can't live here. The people are animals. They'd kill each other for a dollar. I work fourteen hours a day and save my money. I'll save up a little more and go home to Palestine. But there they shoot guns. They don't shoot guns where you live, right?"

"No."

We pay, say good-bye, and leave. I roll out of the store. I turn the wheelchair around and look through the shop window at the elderly Palestinian. A fortunate man. He has a homeland.

Freedom

San Francisco. The city of my dreams, a place of human habitation in the capitalist hell. A city of oddballs and outcasts.

I am out on the sidewalk. It is my last day in America. Tomorrow they are taking me to the airport and putting me back on the plane. The plane will get me to Russia before my visa runs out. There, in faraway Russia, they will put me carefully on the couch and sentence me to life imprisonment within four walls. Kind Russian people will give me food and drink vodka with me. I will have plenty to eat, and I will probably be warm. I will have everything there but freedom. They will bar me from seeing the sun, roaming through the city, sitting in a café. They will explain condescendingly that all these excesses are for normal, full-fledged citizens. They will give me a little more food and vodka and remind me again of my black ingratitude. They will say I want too much, that I need to be patient a little longer, just a little longer, fifty years or so. I will agree to everything they say and nod, detached. I will obediently do as I am told and silently endure the disgrace and humiliation. I will accept my inferiority as an inevitable evil and start wasting away slowly. And when I get sick of this bastard life and ask for some poison, I will, of course, be refused. A quick death is forbidden in that distant and humane country. All they'll let me do is slowly poison myself with vodka in hopes of a stomach ulcer or a heart attack.

I am out on the sidewalk. If I push the throttle as far as it will go, the electric wheelchair's powerful motor will carry me off into the unknown. The plane will fly without me. In a couple of days, the wheelchair battery will run out of charge. I won't survive in this harsh and magnificent country without money or papers. The most I can count on is another day of freedom, and then—death.

———— ◆ ————

This is America. Here everything is sold, and everything is bought—a terrible, cruel country. You can't count on compassion. But I had my fill of compassion back in Russia. I am okay with ordinary business.

This is America.

"What's for sale?"

One day of my freedom. Real freedom. Sun and air. Couples are kissing on the park benches. A hippie is strumming the guitar. The right to see one more time how a little girl is feeding a squirrel from her hand. For the first and only time in my life, I will see a city at night and the blaze of thousands of headlights. For the last time, admire the neon signs and dream of the unachievable happiness of being born in this marvelous country. The real deal, the very best quality. Made in America.

"How much does it cost?"

"A little less than life."

"I'll take it. Keep the change."

———— ◆ ————

Later, in Russia, I drank vodka from dawn to dusk for an entire month, crying through the nights, and in my drunken delirium, trying to feel the joystick of my non-existent mythical wheelchair. And every day, I regretted making the wrong choice at the decisive moment.

Novocherkassk

I was born in Moscow. Moscow is the capital of Russia. In school, we knew everything about Moscow. We sang about Moscow and recited poems. We were told that Moscow was the best, the most beautiful city in the world. I don't know, I have only passed through Moscow and St. Petersburg as well. I am not about to argue. It may very well be that everything they told us was the truth. Maybe that's how it is. Lots of people are sure of that – at least, the Muscovites are.

I have seen three world cities with my own eyes: Novocherkassk, Berkley, and Madrid. But first, there was Novocherkassk.

I had known about Novocherkassk for a long time. Legends were told about Novocherkassk. People said that at the Novocherkassk children's home, they ate potatoes every day, winter and summer. They said tomatoes grew in Novocherkassk. And not just tomatoes. Apricots, watermelons, and cantaloupes grew in that fairy tale city, walnuts and corn, sweet peppers, and squash. I had tried all these things a couple of times in my life, and I had read that these fruits and vegetables grew in the south. I looked for Novocherkassk on a geographical map of the world, so I knew this city was in the south of Russia. People also said that those who couldn't walk at all were taken to Novocherkassk, to the home for the elderly and the disabled. A three-story brick building. You could ride around in wheelchairs, they had attendants and doctors there, people lived for a long time there, and no one died immediately. Of course, all this seemed like a fairy tale, a fiction, an impossible dream. What of it, though? I believed in Novocherkassk. I had to; I had to believe in something.

Sometimes dreams do come true. An ordinary lottery ticket turns into a pile of cash, fern blossoms and a fairy godmother flies down to help an orphan. One fine, incredible, impossible day, a very important man in Moscow signed a very important piece of paper, and they moved me to Novocherkassk. Everything I had so naively believed in turned out to be the truth, even potatoes and apricots.

I am young and relatively healthy. I hope to see many more world cities. I'll see Paris and Tokyo, Rome and Sydney, Buenos Aires and Berkley. I absolutely must see Berkley again. I believe that all these cities do, in fact, exist in the world. I believe it the way I once believed in Novocherkassk.

I was born in Moscow. I was very unlucky to be born in that terrible, insane city. I was lucky in Novocherkassk. Novocherkassk is a good city. I would have died if Russia didn't have a Novocherkassk.

Black

As always in life, black and white alternate, and disappointment follow success. Everything changes. Everything must change. That's the way it's supposed to be; that's how things work. I know this, I am not against it, I can only hope. I hope for a miracle. I sincerely wish, passionately want my black stripe to last a little longer, not to change to a white one.

I don't like white. White is the color of impotence and doom, the color of hospital ceilings, and white sheets. Insured care and care, silence, peace, nothing. The everlasting nothing of hospital life.

Black is the color of struggle and hope. The color of the night sky, the confident and clear backdrop of dreams, the temporary lulls between the white, the endless daytime periods of my bodily infirmities. The color of dreams and fairy tales, the color of the inner world behind my closed eyes. The color of freedom, the color I chose for my electric wheelchair.

And when my turn comes to go down the line of impersonal, well-meaning mannequins in white lab coats and I reach my end, my very own eternal night, I will leave behind only letters. My letters. My black letters on a white background. I hope.

ABOUT THE AUTHOR

Rubén David González Gallego is a Russian writer and journalist. Rubén was born in USSR without the use of his hands and feet. The official diagnosis is cerebral palsy. The Soviet officials have told his mother that the child has died and sent him to a state orphanage. Rubén spent his childhood in orphanages and nursing homes of the Soviet Union.

In 2001, when he was 33 years old, he met his mother for the first time at a conscious age. Rubén traveled around Europe and the world. He lived in the German Freiburg, Spanish Madrid. In the mid-2000s, he left for the United States.

He is an author of three books. The "White on Black" is his first one. In 2003 he received one of the most prestigious national literary awards, "Booker—Open Russia."

Now Rubén, his wife, and daughter are living in Israel.

Made in the USA
Monee, IL
08 December 2020